A Book of Kells

Growing Up in an Ego Void

To Leslie, Paula, Alexandra and all the family's children

A Book of Kells
Growing Up in an Ego Void

Cookstown Farm, 1912

Margaret Kell Virany

AMICUS No. 28047642
Monograph
NLC COPIES: NL Stacks – FC27 V47 A3 2002
NUMBERS: Canadiana: 20030032091
CLASSIFICATION: LC Class no.: FC27*
Dewey: 920.72/0971 21
SUBJECT: Virany, Margaret Kell -- Family
Children of clergy -- Canada -- Biographies

Virany & Virany Desktop Publishers,
478 Du Caveau Street, Gatineau,
Québec, J9H 5N7
Amazon.com or Amazon.ca: Margaret Kell Virany: Books
ISBN 0-9699142-1-0
ISBN-13: 978-0969914211

Visit www.booksurge.com to order additional copies.

A Book of Kells
Growing Up in an Ego Void

Fairbank Church, 1934

Contents

William and Mary Kell, c. 1890

Acknowledgments

Our family name, Kell, comes from the Greek word, keltoi, which is usually translated as Celts. In 500 B.C. they were the dominant tribe populating Europe north of the Mediterranean Sea.

This memoir, *A Book of Kells*, tells the story of descendants of William and Mary Kell, who came to this continent in the 1850's and tried, as Methodists, to illuminate the gospels in their daily lives. The original *Book of Kells* is considered to be the most beautifully illuminated gospel manuscript in western civilization. It was created by a community of monks living in Kells, Ireland, in the ninth century. The Kells Round font on the cover of this book imitates their work and biblical references throughout are italicized.

"Ego void" is my attempt to describe the all-absorbing atmosphere of the beautifully altruistic, redemptive, Utopian, Christian myth. Good souls existed devoid of ego.

It was Elspeth Butterworth and her school class here in Aylmer who bolstered me to the point where I dared write this book. Then my eldest sister Tanis poured her heart and soul into the concept of a story about our parents "for all people and all time". My middle sister Enid, generous, fair, loyal, organized and supportive, offered memories, pictures, financial help and balance.

Long-ago personal and printed recollections flowed from my mother's Sunday School pupil Dorothy Letton, my mother's first cousin Lois Hicks and my father's eldest niece Mary Dunlop. Dr. Taylor Statten Jr. shared material about his father;

John Ross about his mother and Robert Meikle about Norway House and canoeing in northeastern Manitoba.

Distinguished, knowledgeable friends and colleagues in the Media Club of Ottawa helped with their expertise -- particularly Olive Patricia Dickason on the Swampy Cree and Valerie Knowles on Canadian historical data.

The manuscript was made fit to print only with the rallying-round of immediate family members. My tv-director daughter Paula edited it; her feedback and suggestions from the younger generation sparked improvements. My teacher daughter Alexandra insisted that I not trust my own final proofreading. Then I drafted my ever-helpful husband Thomas into this role and he found another 70 errors!

In my most appreciated rejection letter out of many from publishing houses, Dilshad Engineer of Oberon Press inserted advice on structure which I took. Then BookSurge, a state-of-the-art internet company based in Charleston, South Carolina and (until 2005) Vancouver, B.C., produced the final product to great satisfaction.

In 2003 A Book of Kells was featured along with others in the BookSurge booth at the Frankfurt Book Fair. Clues on how to change vital details in order to meet Canadian as well as international standards of promotion and appearance were gleaned from Timothy Staveteig, Publisher of Pilgrim Press, and acted on in the second edition (2005).

This third edition happily, belatedly, pays my acknowledgments to those by whom I feel loved, others who helped me anyway and all who give me reason to be extremely grateful.

The Author

Introduction

Looking For My Parents' Lost Egos

It was a simple matter of hunkering down cross-legged in a circle of South Hull School students to read from my mother's journals during Heritage Week. As I evoked the adventures of a girlish idealist from nineteen-twenties England, the wide-eyed silence around me began to tug not only at my throat but at some deeper place. The huge aspirations and boundless faiths that crossed the ocean with my parents' lives had crashed upon rocky northern shores, where ancestral totems had held sway for eons and aboriginals appeased capricious gods. I saw that primordial need to know who we are and not to be alone rising up in the children's trusting eyes. This moment of story-telling was far more than an afternoon, it was the impetus of a book.

After all, I couldn't leave my parents alone forever as if it were really they who lay dead and buried underneath the tombstone engraved with their names. They expected more. They spent their lifetimes prepping in gentle terms for what was to come, not presuming to know what its precise nature would be. Once Mother said ruefully that she had "become a legend". Father was loath to pack "the body" off to the undertaker and sought comfort in a last-ditch attempt to direct one more significant, symbolic gesture to the world -- his own funeral.

My parents lived past ninety years of age and provoke smiles and queries long after their interment in the Kell cemetery plot at Cookstown, Ontario. As children being brought up in different parts of the world, they both had the same idea. They would devote their lives to being a good example for others. This is a rather risky career path. It meant not taking credit themselves for the things they did but giving it to God.

To put the dilemma in grand terms, just as Faust made a bargain with the Devil and lost his soul, can one make a pact with God and lose one's ego? And if such a dedicated couple fall in love and get married, are the children of their union ego-challenged too?

The after-life was the tacit goal and focus of the household my parents set up. On the one hand, they observed a disciplined, peaceful, perfect pattern, devoid of ego. On the other, they couldn't stop bickering. She nagged, he withdrew, nobody smiled or laughed. As a child plunked down in this atmosphere, I found the paradoxes perplexing. The everlasting was approached through written words and meditation. Practical life was tackled with hard work and obstinacy. We never talked. Life had two tracks but only one manual. But how could the Bible help me figure out how to twist a knob and open a door?

As I grew up, I went my own way, salvaging what I could from my perceived fate of having inexplicable, albeit decent, parents. They dropped a few tell-tale signs, like bear skins and tennis racquets, and I suspected they hadn't always been so miserable. I wished I could find out what was really them, not an example of something better.

Some years after they were gone, my sister, Tanis, gave me a metal box containing Mother's papers and elected me "most likely to write a family history." Not until I was telling the grade four class in South Hull School that today's journal is tomorrow's heritage, did I twist the tiny key dangling from the lock. I read one page out loud and passed the journal around so the children could see Mother's handwriting from seventy years before. A penciled note explained that the splotches were made by drips from the paddle that was propelling her. I read some more pages about a winter cariole ride at -40 degrees and the children sat enthralled. Within seconds, Mother's long-ago, tender story was in danger of being splotched again, this time by my tears.

With Mother's box now in hand, and Father's diaries and lantern slides, I began my search to unravel mysteries. For one thing, why had she not let him have one of her chocolates the week before he died, even though he begged her for it?

Part I

Early Recollections

Atlantic Ocean, 1937

I

Kell and Ward Comings Into the World

I was born in Cookstown, Ontario, on July 18, 1933, and am very grateful my parents were holidaying at the farm. Otherwise, the name of the place where we lived, Lemonville, would appear on my birth certificate. All my life I have tried to avoid being a lemon. The first memory I have is of looking out from behind bars and feeling very, very good about myself. This was somewhat before I learned the sobering truth that the self has to be put away in order to save the immortal soul, which needs redeeming. I like to imagine that somebody came to my crib, patted me on the head and said I was a pretty baby. My parents weren't normally demonstrative when I was awake, but they might have made an exception when they thought I was asleep. I have always had a very strong feeling they loved me.

My birth was not as exuberant as my Father's at the Kells' Clover Hill farm in Cookstown on July 23, 1897. JACK (an acronym) arrived when the neighboring farmers were gathered to help with the harvest. Two steam engines which had been pulled up the lane by two teams of horses blew their whistles from a stop at the top of the ramp leading into the upper level of the barn. Their wheels were connected by belts to the wheels of the threshing machine on a heavy platform inside and a pile of golden grain descended into waiting bushels. Now there would be wheat to take to the mill for flour, grain for the hens and ducks, oats for the horses and barley for the pigs. The machine also spewed out a separate pile of straw to make mattresses. To-night the children would stuff their new ticks full and bounce up and down on them with glee. In the midst of this commotion, a bonanza of a baby boy came into the world. His mother's face bore the lines of hard work and stern truths but this child's free spirit would flower in harmony with the providential God of their beautiful, self-sufficient farm. My grandma, Mary Jane, had been dismayed to find herself pregnant at age forty-three. She had just given birth to my aunt, Clara, and the two babies would be only eleven months apart in age. How could she possibly cope? Fortunately, my great-aunt, Lovina, volunteered to look after the new baby on her nearby farm. "Your parents wouldn't have kept you if it hadn't been for me," Lovey liked to tease Father, and that made him wince.

Father was named John after his father, Ambrose after a Methodist philanthropist and Campbell after his mother's family. Wee John or The Runt spent much of his early years watching bigger people do things. One day he saw a pedlar at the door burst into tears at the sight of my aunt, Mabel, who looked like the little girl he had left behind in Europe. Mary Jane asked a tramp to churn the butter while she got him something to eat but he turned the handle the wrong way so it came loose and, horrors!, the cream spilled onto the floor. My grandpa, John, sometimes butchered a pig with the help of my uncles, Clifton and Wilson, while Mary Jane made soap out of the fat.

One October day, when Father was six and his sisters were sick, he set out alone in his old straw hat and new red mittens to walk the two miles to school. When some older boys caught up with him and taunted him for his funny outfit, he had to defend his mother's honor (she had knit the mittens) as best he could. However, one of the bullies swung his metal lunchbox and a corner of it gashed Father's chin. In later years, the distinguishing scar on his face was assumed to be a souvenir of hand-to-hand combat in World War I.

Like the rest of their homogeneously Methodist community, the family trotted out by buggy in summer and by cutter in winter to attend church in their Sunday best. Father loved the hymns and Bible stories, although he disliked fairy tales. Jesus made him feel loved and was his real-life hero. His idol (my great-grandfather, William Kell) was a white-haired, erect man who wore a Christie hat to church and never took notice of him. When Father first earned some money, at age eleven, he bought Mary Jane a twelve-pound Waterbury clock and carried it the half mile home from the jewelry store.

Nor was my birth as traumatic as Mother's at home in Portsmouth, England, on Mar. 9, 1900. She was emerging in the breech, with the buttocks coming out first and the head in danger of getting caught. The doctor turned her around with such difficulty that, for some time, she looked like a chicken who had had its neck wrung. Her lifelong complaint of bad nerves perhaps stemmed from this stretching of the spinal cord. Kathleen Elizabeth Ward was a refugee and a survivor, a little lady in need of protection but also a fighter.

When the twins (Enid and Eric) arrived, my grandfather (Walter) woke twenty-two-month-old Mother in the middle of the night. He carried her and dolly down the street, past colored bottles glowing in the chemist's window, to her Wooller grandparents. While my grandmother, Elizabeth, recovered from giving birth, her sisters (a dressmaker, a shop manager and a schoolteacher) doted on Mother. The country was still in mourning for Queen Victoria who had left them all feeling immensely English.

The Bible stories read in Wesley Methodist Chapel's Sunday School gave Mother nightmares of having her arms fall off, like the leper's, or being attacked by lions, like Daniel. Walter had her transferred to a gentler class, where she learned to love all the children in the world and collect pennies for mission work. At age four, she started school and learned how to read, write, sew and knit. She also caught the measles and gave them to the twins. Enid's condition improved but Eric's worsened, so Mother was taken to her Ward grandparents to ride out the crisis. They lived beside the family's bakery, where Walter worked as an accountant. When Mother cried to go home for her sixth birthday, he picked her up. This was just as well because my great-grandmother, Elizabeth Pople Ward, died of a stroke while writing a letter six days later. While there, Mother had become very attached to her and to Winnie, an eight-year-old cousin. When Winnie died five months later of diphtheria, Mother wailed for two days and two nights. In those days childhood diseases took an awful toll.

The J.B. (Jabez Burt) Ward & Sons Bakery, founded on the miracle of baking powder, stood on a busy corner. My great-grandfather's office was linked by a secret door and passageway to his bedroom in the house next door, where he lived with his four unmarried children. Mother's family moved into the house next to his, and my great aunt and uncle, Lottie and Jim Ward, lived on the other side of them. It was all very cozy. Every Saturday, a trusted driver by the name of Bert Trotter delivered Mother via horse-drawn bakery van to spend the day with the Woollers in the old neighborhood.

At age ten, Mother decided privately in church to devote her life to serving Christ and helping others. She was a real help to her cousin, Rupert, the day they went for their first and only visit to a farm. He got kicked in the eye by a horse and Mother was told to run out to the road and hail a bus to take him to hospital. He got better from this accident but, alas, died two years later of diphtheria.

2

Wonderful Whitmore Avenue Where I Get Mad At Mother

When I was eleven months old, we moved to Whitmore Avenue in Fairbank, a district in Toronto. Now there was a real street! I spent moving day howling in a playpen on the lawn of the Lemonville parsonage, while the others loaded our belongings onto a moving van. In later years, when I broke into unexplained weepy fits in church, Mother asked me if I thought it was because she had let me cry that day but I said "No." Actually, it wasn't that bad because my sisters (Tanis was five-and-one-half and Enid was three and-one-half) tell me they jumped in and out of the playpen to try to amuse me.

In later years, I recognized Whitmore Avenue when I went to see the opera Carmen. In the opening scene, she and the other working girls pour out of the cigarette factory into a pageant of activity. This too was a vibrant, working-class neighborhood. From its hiding-place somewhere past the end of our street, the whistle of the Patten & Baldwin knitting mill sounded four times a day: "Get to work, eat lunch, get back to work, go home." The workers flowed past our house to and from the street-car stop at the corner of Eglinton Avenue and Dufferin Street. These Tillie the Toilers wore overalls, tied their hair up in colorful kerchiefs and carried brown paper lunch bags, just as in the comic strip. They chatted and shifted their way along, three abreast, as the narrow sidewalk forced one or the other to step off the curb or onto a lawn. The odd male employee took the other side of the street and stared straight ahead as he strode purposefully along, swinging his black metal lunch box.

Whitmore was a street of many marvels. Before we got up, the milkman's wagon trotted by bringing bottles of fresh milk to replace the empties everyone set out on the front steps. Once a week, Baker Tommy arrived dressed in his brown uniform and cap with yellow trim, which matched the writing on his bread wagon. A retinue of tousled kids and nosing canines came with him, fussing over his blinkered, dapple-gray horse while Tommy loaded up his flat basket. Mother was ready at the back door for his cheery words and her order of "one white and one brown." She managed the food and housekeeping on $30 a month and told us the cup cakes and butter tarts were "just for looking." She saved our stale bread and turned it into a simpler treat by adding an egg, milk, sugar and raisins to create bread pudding. Occasionally, if company was coming and she hadn't had time to bake, we got a jelly roll. This was the Depression and no one had money to spare. But the children of women who were as smart as my mother didn't suffer and even felt rich.

Great excitement erupted when the bell on the knife-sharpener's grinder wheel was heard coming up the street. Housewives yelled down from the windows and then rushed out with their knives and scissors. One of the street's regular visitors frightened me; I was glad to be kept indoors when the sheenyman (junk dealer) came. His decrepit, creaking wagon was filled with weird objects and pulled by a skinny nag. He had hollow eyes and a scraggy, gray beard and pleaded in sepulchral (I'd heard that word in church) tones for "rags, bones and bottles."

Enid and I were glued to the livingroom window when the Belle Ewart Ice Company truck drove up. She demonstrated her superior knowledge by reading the name out for me: "Belly Wart." The iceman used a leather strap to carry a dripping block of ice around to the back stoop and chiseled it with his pick until it fit into the ice box. When the season changed, the coal delivery truck came instead. Two men who were black with coal dust from head to toe emptied bags of "anthracite" in through a side basement window, which was actually a coal chute. Father loved to dignify things with big words.

A car traveling on Whitmore Avenue was a rare event but one day, when my legs still weren't very long, I decided to do a physics experiment. I saw a car coming down our street and was sure I could run across the street from the point where I was before it got to the point in the middle of the road which we both would cross. Mother was just a few feet away but she wasn't expecting me to take off like a shot. The car came screeching to a halt and, before I knew it, Mother was helping the most white-faced man I have ever seen in my life into the house and reviving him with a cup of tea. So much for physics.

We learned to tell the time and picked up street savvy by contracting with Mother to let us out. We could look at the men building the house on the vacant lot, if we promised to be back in ten minutes. We could ride up and down on the sidewalk, Enid on her tricycle and I on my kiddie car, but just in front of two houses in either direction. We learned to sing the irreverent ditty:

I love coffee, I love tea
I love the boys and the boys love me
Tell your mother to hold her tongue
She had a fella when she was young
Tell your father to do the same
He is the one who changed her name.

We reported back to Mother that you could buy a "grab-bag" of broken candies and gum for a penny at the corner store, the father from two doors down was in jail and you could take dancing lessons. One enviable girl had a kilt and another had tap-dancing shoes. One day, my sisters brought me home from the vacant lot dripping with blood after I sat on a piece of rusty tin to watch the older children bob-skate on a frozen puddle.

Mother scarcely stepped out into the street and could hardly wait until the new parsonage was built. Our piano crate was left in the backyard as a playhouse—until she found a hobo sleeping in it and being fed by Father. Once he talked her into going to Ottawa and leaving us with a baby-sitter, against her better judgment. When they returned, they caught us in the headlights of the car, dancing in the street in our nighties at 10 p.m.

While we were having a ball on Whitmore Avenue, Father was saddened and Mother unnerved by the deaths of his two brothers. In 1931 Clifton had fallen through an opening concealed by hay in the top floor of the barn and hit his head on the concrete floor below. Mother was staying at the farm at the time and could see he had concussion but no one else seemed overly concerned. Then, in the winter of 1933, Wilson slipped on an icy, cement step while carrying a load of feed into the barn and hit the back of his head. He was operated on to remove a brain tumor but died in 1934 at age forty-nine. Clifton was fifty-one when he died, also of a brain tumor, in 1936.

Mother was treated like a queen, I guessed because she was from England. Father took her breakfast in bed on Sunday mornings and when she had a headache. He had been brought up on a farm and was better qualified to do the dirty work, such as digging and hoeing the vegetable garden, cleaning our shoes, stoking the furnace and making porridge. Giving us our Saturday night baths and inserting enemas were also his duties. He was gentle; I used to ask him to rub me up and down with the bath towel as we chanted "Rub-a-dub-dub" together, to my great delight.

One day, I was wearing my new sweater when Enid began to tease me with a pair of little scissors. She kept opening and closing them, coming closer and closer and saying "I'm going to cut your sweater. I'm going to cut your sweater." The more she did this, the more desperate I became, crying "Don't tut my fweater! Don't tut my fweater!" She was so amused she couldn't resist and cut just one little stitch in the center front. Now Mother took notice and called Father down from his study to administer swift justice. He put Enid in the broom closet and shut the door. I was devastated to hear my high-spirited sister's muffled sobs. She never cried. She was my best friend and de facto mother who blew my nose, dried my tears, gave me a hug and pulled up my pants. This was the closest we ever came to having a crucifixion in our house. I was very relieved when she got out.

When guests came to visit and Mother had to make bright conversation, she told them that Tanis had been born on an Indian reservation and her name was taken from the Cree word for daughter. Enid was named after Aunt Enid who lived in Australia and was a twin. As for me, she would say, "Margaret was supposed to have been red-haired twin boys but, of course, we are very glad to have her." I felt my ego falling down like my bloomers did when the elastic was loose. Why couldn't she have said, "This is our brown-haired, brown-eyed little girl of whom we are so proud?" I was so mad at Mother I stopped letting her touch me. Whenever she tried, I pushed her away.

Mother and I only got along when she said it would help her headache if I played with her hair. It was short (Father cut all our hair) and gray, parted at the side and anchored with a huge bobbypin; she made no attempt to look like the mothers in her knitting books who had colored hair and permanent waves. Father had his hair done properly at the barber and took his white shirts and clerical collars to the Chinese laundry, since Mother flatly refused to iron them. Anyway, she liked to lean back in the livingroom armchair with her eyes shut while I mounted the attack, on behalf of vanity, with an arsenal of hairpins, bobbypins, barrettes, combs, clips, ribbons and elastic bands.

Sylvia Brown lived across the street in a single-family house which contained curlers, housecoats, slippers and an Eaton Beauty doll—things you could buy for money. "Money" was seldom mentioned in our house, although Father took me to the bank and showed me a savings account book, signature and check. I'd heard that *it is easier for a camel to go through the eye of a needle than for a rich man to get into heaven* so I had my reservations. I made up my mind I'd never let a lack of mere money stand between me and whatever I wanted to do with my life.

Father got me out of Mother's hair by taking me along to make visits in tar-papered houses on Glencairn Avenue and to drop off food and bundles of clothing at a depot at City Limits on Yonge Street. We were fortunate that Father had a regular salary of $1100 a year, as well as a free house (we paid for the heating, telephone and car.)

When Mother was young, all the Wards gathered on Christmas Day to eat around a heavily-laden table and then attend the matinée puppet show at the Theatre Royal. Afterwards, Jabez told his tales of South Africa, where he had made his fortune in produce and diamonds. Mother loved to hear how he sent for Great-grandmother to come out from England and be his companion for life. He waited on the dock with a minister so they could get married the moment she arrived. He saw her ship come into view but then it got blown out to sea for another three weeks.

In the Cookstown house Mary Jane and Mabel bought after Clifton died, the floors were covered with linoleum, the kitchen table with oil-cloth, the walls with soldiers' pictures and the window sills with plants. Polly, the parrot, talked a blue streak and whistled for Towser, the dog, to come running. We drank water from a well and relieved ourselves in the unheated "attachment" beyond the back kitchen. It boasted two holes to sit on and an Eaton's catalogue hanging on a wire hook. The night before Christmas, Enid and I tried to fall asleep in a big, four-poster bed under layers of home-made quilts but were too excited. We stared up at the stovepipe holes plugged with round metal plates decorated with painted flowers, listening for the sound of Santa's reindeer on the tin roof. A porcelain basin and pitcher of water stood on a cherrywood washstand with a potty concealed behind its lower-cupboard doors. By a miracle, we dropped off and, when we awoke, found the stockings at the foot of our bed stuffed with an orange, a candy cane, crayons and a handkerchief. More presents lay under the tree to be unwrapped on Christmas morning, while the stuttering king (a real case for Christian compassion) gave his radio address. We had worn red, white and blue dresses to a picnic to celebrate his Coronation in the summertime.

When we stayed home for Christmas, Mother made pink-and-green potato candy and coconut balls and sent Father to the butcher's to buy suet for carrot pudding. Mince tarts, shortbread, jelly, cranberry sauce, pickles, fancy cookies, lemonade and blanched almonds sharing a divided dish with sultana raisins appeared on Christmas Day, or if company came. She never flaunted the tastes she was born to but taught us, as Christians, to be grateful God gave us food in whatever guise.

The Santa Claus who supposedly came down the chimney soon became suspect in our house. Father considered he was horning in on another man's birthday. Not only were fairy tales a side issue in his view of things but he resented mercenary interests trying to usurp a religious event. From the pulpit he told the story of the original Nicholas, the 14th-century Russian saint who gave gifts to the poor. When a ridiculous, pillow-stuffed Santa romped in as the climax to our church Christmas concerts, Father nudged the older children to guess who he really was. One year he put his old spats into Tanis's Christmas stocking as a joke.

3

Off To Portsmouth Where Father's Ship
Once Came In

Early in 1937, the mailman delivered a letter which caused Mother to hoot and wave it around like a flag. We were going to go to England on a big boat! Sailing was in our family, I knew. Mother wore a sailor hat and coat when she was my age and Father kept a bosun's whistle in his study drawer, along with pencil stubs and a penknife. Father's history of sailing, however, did not occur under happy circumstances.

The First World War broke out in 1914 when Father was in his last year at Barrie Collegiate. He was boarding with the family of his friend, Ezra Parkhouse, and busy with math, history, sciences, English, Latin, literary society, school newspaper and debates. (One topic was "Resolved that the liquor trade is worse than war.") Social life revolved around the church, picnics and skating. All male students were issued the khaki uniforms of the Cadet Corps and drilled regularly. Then came the day when they marched to the railway station to see "the boys" off, including their favorite teacher.

Father and Clifton signed up at a patriotic meeting but John said "No" to Father; he had to stay on the farm. For nineteen months, while the Parliament Building in Ottawa burned and Clifton fought overseas in the trenches, Father hayed, hoed, hauled, chopped trees, sawed wood, shoveled manure, repaired fences, dug up potatoes, took cattle and pigs to market, picked beans and disked with four horses at a time.

He told himself that a man in the most humble place could be a credit to the worth and dignity of the human race. A work horse got no glory but was just as valuable as a race horse who made the headlines at Fort Erie. The Runt grew into a strong, 163-lb, five foot ten inch man.

Father and his pals, Bill Orchard and Ezra Parkhouse, saw a poster-sailor looking them in the eye, pointing and saying "Help Britannia Rule the Waves." They took a train to Toronto to enlist in the Royal Navy Canadian Volunteer Reserve (RNCVR.) Never mind that news of fatalities was pouring in, their teacher had been killed or that farmers were exempt. It was the sporting thing to do and quite a deal. No experience was necessary. You just needed to be the son of a natural-born British subject and between the ages of eighteen and thirty-eight. You got a free kit, free uniform, free trip abroad, sweethearts kissing you good-bye, military bands playing and $1.10 a week in pay.

The brutal truth behind the posters was that German submarines had sunk one-hundred and sixty-nine British merchant ships, not just combat ships, in one month. The Kaiser was barring the seas and cutting England off from the rest of the world and all her allies. The British responded by building forty-eight trawlers and one hundred drifters for anti-submarine work and put out a call for enlistees. Seventeen hundred Canadians came to the aid of a motherland in distress.

When they parted, John told Father he would never see him again but Father assured him he would be all right. He and his two pals took a train to Halifax and were assigned to the Niobe, a hugely-armed, retired British cruiser tied up in the harbor. They got drafts and crossed the ocean on Apr. 18, 1917, four days after Clifton bore soldiers away on stretchers from the front line of the final, victorious assault against the Germans at Vimy Ridge. He jumped into a trench just before a bomb exploded and barely survived. The 3,589 dead and 6,000 wounded Canadians he fought alongside were not so lucky.

In the Portsmouth barracks, the three buddies learned how to swim, attended seamanship school and read Knights in Armour by Edward Woods. This little book glorified the virtues of courage, chivalry, purity and loyalty and urged them to have an indomitable fighting spirit against all odds. One day, outside the Sailors' Rest, they saw a sign inviting colonial servicemen to come to the Young Men's Bible Class at Wesley Methodist Chapel. This huge church, complete with four bathrooms and a four-story extension for meetings, stood on the edge of the Portsea slums where John Wesley once preached. Father, Ezra and Bill attended the next Sunday and received a warm welcome from Mr. Ward, the teacher, who invited them to his home for Sunday tea. They followed his footsteps over an intricate brick path and came back the same way for the evening service.

As an "ordinary" seaman, Father spent three seasick months patrolling the English Channel, sweeping for mines and chasing submarines. The routine of round-the-clock watches and meager meals was cheered by shore leave every ten days and by letters and parcels from home—particularly from Suzy Shier, the doctor's daughter. But one letter from Cookstown was so painful to write that Father's Sunday School teacher was given the task. She informed him that his dear Pa, age fifty-nine, had died and been buried a month ago. John had been picking apples from a tree when a limb on which his ladder was resting broke. A sharp twig pierced his clothing and punctured his lung, and peritonitis set in. Father and Clifton spent a week's leave together in Yorkshire, visiting a cousin whom John had found before he died. She lived in Woodmansey and helped them find more relatives near Market Weighton. Clifton even met a girl he wanted to marry.

My great-grandparents, William and Mary Kell, had emigrated to Canada in 1850 when he was a simple farm foreman, unable to afford a Christie hat like the one Father remembers him wearing. They had a difficult time and had three children, one of whom died in infancy. Their luck changed in 1855 when Mary received a letter informing her that a legacy was waiting for her to pick up in Pocklington, England, in person. A legal firm had located her through an estate notice in the Toronto newspaper. It sought a "Mary Faulkner, married to a man named Kell, living in Canada." Thomas Clifton, a Yorkshire gentleman, had revealed in his will that he had had a secret love child who had been adopted by the Faulkner family. He wanted to look after her by leaving her one thousand pounds, a very large sum. William and Mary borrowed money from Faulkner relatives in Canada and made the ocean trip to claim their fortune. Shortly after they returned, John was born.

They kept this story to themselves because of the disgrace of an upper class gentleman having had an affair with the butcher's daughter. The folk who flocked to hear Methodist circuit preachers would have been scandalized to know my devout great-grandmother was illegitimate. In later years, John and Mary Jane named their first son Clifton, after the benevolent skeleton in the closet. They named their second son Wilson, after the man who sold William and Mary property at Cherry Creek (just south of Churchill, Ontario) where they had a handsome brick house built.

By the time Father was re-assigned to a sweeper on the Bristol Channel and North Sea, he had been to the Wards' for tea several times and attended the Christmas At Home at Wesley Chapel with them. He had given his witness to Christ in the Young Men's Bible Class and bonded with Walter. Father wrote to Eric from Swansea saying he would miss them. It was Enid who replied and she and Father started writing to each other.

The British put guns on everything that could float, as German U-boats sought to destroy all allied vessels. Gunnery Officer Kell advanced to "able" and then "leading" seaman. He was assigned to the Lapageria to patrol the Bristol Channel between Ilfracombe, Hartland Point and Caldy Island, escorted by the Captain Pollen and the Houbara. Mortal danger lurked unseen below and close by but a little levity surfaced. One day, the sailors on the All's Well, a patrol ship, gave them some fresh fruit. Another day, Father's ship dropped a depth charge after the Captain Pollen sank a German sub and the sailors celebrated by picking up fish out of the debris. The war news was bad, with the Germans taking 70,000 prisoners on the western front.

Eighty-nine British minesweepers were blown up by the enemy in 1917 but they took in a haul of 4,700 mines.

By June, 1918, Clifton had survived two bullets in his helmet and three wounds to his limbs and was discharged to run the family farm. He went to pick up the girl he had fallen in love with in Yorkshire but she had a cold. He jumped to the conclusion that she wouldn't be able to stand the Canadian climate and didn't propose to her. This was too bad because he never did get married.

Father, Ezra and Bill were drafted back to Halifax and were shocked to find the city of 50,000 decimated. A mile-high explosion, the worst in history, had leveled the northern, industrial end of the city, destroying 1600 buildings and killing 1600 people. Sections of the Niobe had been blasted away. In December the Imo, a Belgian relief vessel, and the Mont Blanc, a French munitions carrier, had collided in the narrowest part of the harbor. Sailors from the Niobe were sent in a rowboat to pull the burning Mont Blanc away from the wooden pier. They didn't know sparks had lit the benzol stored on the ship's deck and the burning liquid was seeping into the holds and igniting 2,766 tons of picric acid, TNT and guncotton. All of the sailors perished.

Home on leave for his twenty-first birthday, Father wrote in his diary, "Now I know that I am a failure." He had just read the will left by John, who was ten years old in 1867 when Confederation took place. He valued good citizenship and community and dreamt that his children would be well-educated and help build a strong nation of Canada. He wanted Father to go to university, and left him the money for it, but he felt too restless. Back in Halifax he found all public places, even churches, closed due to the Spanish 'flu epidemic. They re-opened in time for the glorious signing of the Armistice on Nov. 11, 1918. Father joined in the street parade to celebrate the end of the "war to end all wars."

Ernie Taylor (a war services officer with the Halifax YMCA) and Father volunteered to help escort the HMCS Stadacona to the west coast in the spring. They sailed to

Bermuda, Jamaica, Panama, Costa Rica, Mexico, California and crossed the Straits of Juan de Fuca to Victoria with Father at the helm. From Vancouver, they traveled by train across the country, stopping en route at Lake Louise, "the most beautiful place in Canada." Now he was ready to get on with his life. He went home to the farm to help with the harvest and then enrolled in the class of '23 at Victoria College at the University of Toronto. He had enlisted in the RNCVR (Royal Navy Canadian Volunteer Reserve) but was discharged from the RCNVR (Royal Canadian Navy Volunteer Reserve.) The name had been changed; Canada was coming into its own in the wake of the Vimy victory and tragedy.

And so it was that, when my sisters and I boarded an ocean-going steamship at the end of June, 1937, we were in the hands of a father who was a veteran of the sea and a mother who was the product of a port. After we landed in England, our heads started swimming with the names of all the relatives we met at Granny Ward's cottage. Our Australian cousins, Patrick, Rory and Bridget, were there and our English cousins, David and Janet.

As we children cavorted on the grass in Granny's rose-arboured garden, there was an undercurrent of grief. The check Grandfather had sent to pay for half of our passage was the last he ever signed. Bakery partner and Sunday school teacher Walter Richard Ward had died at age sixty-five of kidney failure and burn-out from a demanding schedule. As a city councilor, he sat on committees to provide better housing for the poor and combat the spread of venereal disease. As founder and president of the Portsmouth Brotherhood, he was sought after as a guest speaker throughout the country. The Prince of Wales (later King Edward VIII) took an interest in the Brotherhood and, while traveling to France for the funeral of the assassinated president, wrote Walter a letter of good wishes on its thirteenth anniversary. After his death, the Prince donated money to a campaign to raise funds for a cot to be placed in the children's hospital in Walter's memory—and so did a blind beggar. Walter Ward was eulogized as "Rudyard Kipling's ideal man who could walk with both princes and paupers," "a genius of friendship" and "a Peter Pan of a man who never grew old." His name had been proposed for a knighthood by three successive prime ministers but he declined, saying he was better as a plain man.

Most of all, he was Mother's beloved father who read to her when she was little and saved her when she had to flee. She had a memory of him stretched out on the green in front of Rowland's Castle with his head propped up on one hand and elbow, smiling at her and her mother while a birdie pecked at his shoelace. I was sorry he had died before I got a chance to meet him; he has twinkling eyes and a beautiful smile in his picture.

We celebrated my fourth birthday in England with a teddy bear, blanc mange, somersaults and Uncle Eric pulling a rabbit out of a hat and taking moving pictures. Great-uncle Jim offered each of us children a choice of a gold half-sovereign or a chocolate and I took the chocolate. At the London zoo, we rode on an elephant, saw a hippopotamus and a polar bear swimming and watched a chimpanzee tea party. We climbed the Tower of London, saw the changing of the guard at Buckingham Palace and ate tomato sandwiches on a park bench within sight of Big Ben and a beefeater. We bathed and played on a sandy beach on the Isle of Wight and toured Nelson's flagship, the Victory. Mother bought me a sailor doll who looked just like Father did when they first met.

As we crossed the ocean back to Canada on the Empress of Australia, Mother doled out the faintest bit of ego-food by saying we were all good sailors. Our family were the only ones to turn up for dinner when the sea was rough, except for a schoolteacher from Sudbury, Kay Russell. We sent a card to her every Christmas after that. On this cherished trip we were a family of five individuals like any other, not just an institution.

4

That Old Bible and Church Routine For Our Family

Now that we were back home on Whitmore Avenue, things returned to normal (except that we had to go to a hospital and get a nasal spray which protected us against an epidemic of polio which kept the schools closed for a month.) As soon as we finished eating breakfast, Father reached for the Bible on the kitchen window sill, bowed his head and hushed us with a word of prayer. Then either he or Mother read us a passage of scripture. This was followed by a little commentary and a "thought for the day" from the Upper Room booklet, which we took turns reading. Then we shut our eyes and said the Lord's Prayer together. This daily habit gave us food for thought and precepts to follow. We were closely bound together inside a beautiful story of love which defined us.

Father wrote two sermons each week, organized the Sunday School and church services, and looked after the finances. He kept tabs on the mid-week meetings and activities of stewards (the session), elders (the board), choir, young people (YPU), boys (Boys' Brigade), girls (CGIT) and women (WA and WMS.) As pastor to his flock, he was a family counselor, marriage counselor and psychologist. He filled out reports for church headquarters, visited shut-ins and hospital patients and performed marriages, funerals and baptisms. On Sundays, when the venue changed from home to Fairbank United Church, everyone in our family helped him.

My sisters and I accepted that we had been born into the business of setting a good example. It was fun to have a certain identity and importance. The three of us were in the same boat and learned the tricks of the trade. We had Sunday outfits (hand-me-downs in my case) for each season: dress, hat, coat, knee socks, gloves, shoes, hymn book and a purse. Each item was laid out the night before so we wouldn't fight and be late for church. Inside the purse were three pennies tied into the corner of an embroidered handkerchief so they wouldn't drop and clatter. When our parents took us to see the Dionne quintuplets, I compared myself to them enviously. They were on display too but did it with more style, what with ringlets, bows, pastel-colored dresses and shiny tricycles.

Keeping quiet with an appropriate expression on your face for an hour-long, boring service is not easy but at least the hymns are a release. You get to stand on your feet. I improvised alto harmony and picked up good advice from the words. "Jesus Bids Us Shine"—that didn't just mean that you should brush your teeth and hair and shoes, which of course we did, but that you should try to be your very best. "God Sees the Little Sparrow Fall"—what a nice thought. I liked birds too. Mother chose the hymns and played the organ to make sure it was good music. (She liked disciplined tunes, like Welcome Happy Morning, but not body-swaying ones like Ama-az-ing Grace.) She sometimes sat in the choir and sang a solo. The announcements were the best part of the service. You never knew when a Fish Pond, a Strawberry Social, a Bazaar, a Harvest Supper, a Corn Roast, a Hay Ride or a Minstrel Show might be coming up.

The scripture readings went over my head but the gentle lilt of the phrases in the King James version of the Bible was nice and I picked up some fine words, like circumcision and panoply. When Father launched his sermon, we were in for fifteen minutes of serious boredom control. Mother turned around on the organ stool to face us, at this point, and conduct us with her frown. She couldn't really tell if you were clinging to the edge of the pew with both hands while swinging both legs wildly back and forth. You had to be careful not to fall off or kick the pew, and you had to use your elbows to fend off your sisters, who were poking you in the ribs. If you turned around inconspicuously in your seat enough times, you could find out who was sitting back of you, what their hats looked like and how many people were in church. (The hat was important; Mother took pains to get hers on at just the right angle, smart but not risqué.) When all else failed, you could count the number of pages in the hymn book or try to read it.

Mother put a three-and-one-half pound roast, surrounded with potatoes and vegetables, in the oven before we left for church, in case she wanted to bring someone special home for dinner. I'm not sure how she could afford a roast, since even sausages cost seventeen cents a pound, but Father was good at carving thin slices. The roast lasted until mid-week, when it was taken off the bone, put through the meat-grinder and merged with leftover potatoes, gravy, soup and vegetables in a delicious shepherd's pie. For Sunday supper, we had a can of salmon, lettuce and tomatoes or pickles, potato salad, boiled salad dressing, a jar of cooked fruit and two cookies each. Everything but the salmon was home-made. Mother, being English, knew about fish and said the red sockeye salmon was best. Father grew the vegetables and rhubarb in the backyard; we picked berries by the side of the road on "joy rides" and got apples and eggs when we went to the farm.

Father was a well-meaning, patient man who tried to be *slow to anger and of great mercy*, like the example he was following. He worked hard and never spent money on himself. A corner of my parents' bedroom was his study; the second bedroom was a guest room and the third bedroom was for the three of us. When Father had finished work he would let us type on his typewriter with an old ribbon. His desk faced the back window and his bookcase sagged with dictionaries, encyclopedia, a concordance, a syllabus, a church year-book and books on history, philosophy, theology, law, anthropology, society and psychology. The floor-to-ceiling bookcase in the livingroom housed literary classics.

There was no preaching, religious discussion or praying

for the rest of the day, except to say grace at mealtimes and a personal prayer at bedtime. No one walking into our house would have known it was religious. The only clue was the black-and-white photo of the arched doorway of Victoria College with its engraved biblical motto, *The Truth Shall Make You Free.* Father had gone there to get a BA in English, Philosophy and History and an MA in History. Then he went to Emmanuel College, the other component of Victoria University, to get what was later called a BD in Theology.

But when I walked out of our house I knew we were different, even though Father was good at public relations. When he bought the funeral director's old 1938 Ford V8 to replace our Model T, he sat the neighborhood gang down on the running board and took their picture. Mother, on the other hand, was not. She made us navy blue snowsuits with dunces' hoods out of a kind of wool that little balls of snow clung to. That was embarrassing. During spring cleaning, she showcased her social skills and gave everyone a fright by hanging the bear skins over the sills of the upstairs windows.

As I grew up, I realized that having devotions first thing in the morning was a way to *not have any other gods before me* (Commandment no. 1) and to *honor thy father and mother* (no. 5.) We were *building our home on a rock instead of on sand.* We were repeating a tradition our great-grandparents and grandparents thought was important. When I was a teenager, I begrudged the five or six minutes hijacked from me when I had friends waiting and a school bus to catch. Still, a surprising number of texts stuck in my head and I mulled them over when my mind was idling.

The religion we picked up in our church basement was not always so trustworthy. The non-hierarchical Methodist tradition emphasized listening for the word of God, not looking at icons. Exceptionally, there was a sign up on the church basement wall with three phrases on it arranged one on top of the other. It read, "Christ First; Others Next; Self Last." Someone had lifted the biblical saying *the last shall be first and the first last* and rewritten it in an autocratic, didactic way. These coined words, among the first I ever read and then re-read every Sunday, put me on a false track. There was only one way to interpret them, it seemed to me. The unpoetic text did not invite you to ruminate and gain a variety of insights on how to live. Since I was the youngest and last in the family, I couldn't be spontaneous and playful; I must hold back, be modest and never win at games. This supposed path towards eventual triumph was in fact *betrayal*. Fortunately, wild horses would not have been able to prevent me from doing well at school; I was so eager by the time I got there. Somehow my parents knew that academic ambitions weren't cultivated by directives. All they had to do was expose us to good literature and the words would do the rest.

Many years later, when Tanis and I were comparing notes on what our parents had done to mess us up, we both pointed a finger at that sign. Her maladjustment was that, as the first child in our family, she identified with being Christ. Enid was safe, being always in the middle. When Tanis and I confronted our parents, Mother said, "See, Jack. I told you to take it down." They didn't know who was responsible for the sign; it had been there when we moved to Fairbank. She accused him of being careless and sloughing things off as if they didn't matter. We hadn't wanted to start an argument between our parents but there was no way not to. The more she nagged, the more he got his back up. Yet, to watch him pray earnestly on Sundays for God to "forgive our sins of commission and omission," one knew that he would have changed himself if he could have; so would Mother.

Father's decision to become a minister had germinated as his family knelt in prayer around the breakfast table when he was a little boy. It blossomed when he was a teen-ager attending a religious revival led by famous American evangelists. Then he declared it at a summer camp directed by Canada's foremost boys' work pioneer.

When Hugh T. Crossley and John E. Hunter came to Barrie, the ordinary high school farm boy wouldn't have missed the seventeen consecutive nights of excitement for the world. It was like a rock festival today. The local churches depended on these rallies to keep their members attending for the rest of the year. The stars preached "fire and brimstone" and exhorted the crowd to come up to the rail, cast off their sins and give their lives to Christ. Father didn't get swept up in the over-emotionalism because he didn't believe in heaven and hell. What loving father would condemn a person to eternal punishment? However, he did think a man could choose a wrong path and end up in a hell of his own making. He and his pals were good boys who had no quarrels with their families' religious ways. Reading Harry Emerson Fosdick's The Manhood of the Master convinced him that the core message of the gospel was that Jesus was not so much a miracle-worker as a man of compassion.

When Taylor Statten, national boys' work secretary of the YMCA, saw boys heading off to war in 1914, he decided to develop a challenging program to keep them at home. His system of charts, certificates, awards and badges became the Canadian Standard Efficiency Tests. The Protestant Sunday Schools joined with the YMCA to teach this program to hundreds of thousands of boys. Church congregations sponsored promising youths to spend a week at a summer camp and Father was chosen.

Statten loved the north woods as passionately as did his friend, the artist Tom Thomson. He learned about nature and the ways of the native peoples from his mentor, the author Ernest Seton, and he thought up the idea of adapting the Indian council ring to summer camping. With some of the flamboyance of his distant cousin, circus-founder P.T. Barnum, Statten and his wife dressed in full Plains Indian regalia and gave themselves Indian names.

At the camp, Father adopted for his own life pattern the Fourfold Design for Young People. It was based on the text, *And Jesus increased in wisdom and stature and in favor with God and man*. A boy should (1) get as much education as possible (2) keep his body fit and not abuse it with intemperate eating or drinking (3) seek God's favor on his life, and (4) work well with his fellow citizens and be socially minded. On the last day of the camp, the Chief interviewed each boy and asked him what he wanted to be. Father replied, "A minister."

He was fulfilling his father's own dream. John, at age fifteen, had decided to become a Methodist minister but William had furrowed his brow under his Christie hat and told the local minister, "No, not John. He is too good a worker." Instead, he bought him Clover Hill farm. He turned into an excellent agriculturist, producing some of the best crops in the area.

After Father's decision to become a minister, Cookstown United Church commissioned him at a special service before he went off to study. The guest speaker for the occasion said it would be a fatal flaw for a person entering this career to ask, "What's in it for me?" Giving up self-interest is a tall order for a normal, sane, practical man but Father wanted to live a life of service to God. In the margin of his diary, he asked which would help humanity more: preaching a certain set of beliefs or setting a good example in one's daily life? His life's answer was "Both." As a professional minister, he had to do the former while, in his heart, he was committed to the latter.

I did have a beautiful party on my sixth birthday. Three playmates sat with me and my sisters at a table by the side of the garage where a row of pink hollyhocks were in bloom. I had not yet decided what I would be. Thoughts of becoming a minister had been put on hold since Easter when I wrote a sermon with the title, Why is Good Friday Called Good? My thesis was that it should be renamed Black Friday. I wrote out four copies and delivered them to homes along the other side of the street. Mrs. Brown ran over and showed her copy to Mother and they both gave me quizzical looks. I could see by the way my mother disowned my behavior that blaring out one's religion was not to be done. I would have to find some other way of becoming a leader. What a United Church minister's daughter learned at home did not slide easily into a slot on the street but I loved them both.

5

Mother's Fit Terrifies Me But the Pattern Comes To the Rescue

Let me go back to a Monday morning in the fall of 1938, when Enid and Tanis were away at school, so I was the only one at home and it was very quiet. Mother was looking gray and fatigued from the day before. She had on her big cardigan, which looked like it was made out of rope and had big pockets to hold the men's handkerchiefs she needed when her nose was red and dripping. She got out the box of soap, which made her sneeze, and called Father to roll out the wringer washing machine from its storing place off the kitchen. He filled up the rinsing tubs placed on wooden stools, while she sorted the mound of dirty clothes and linens. I don't know what precipitated it but all of a sudden she lit into him with her tongue.

'Everything was his fault. She labored and slaved for him. She did not get any pay. She did not get any of the glory and fun he got, standing up in the pulpit and going to all the young peoples' parties. It was all very well that he helped her on Monday mornings, putting the clothes through the wringer and helping her twist the sheets dry, but where was he when the cleaning lady got sick and all the meals had to be prepared and he expected her to have meetings and weddings in the house and entertain visiting ministers? When was the last time he took her out for dinner or to a concert or a play? And what about the new fur-collared coat Mabel had bought herself? Did he expect her to go around like his mother, in a slip made out of the flowered material from an old dress hanging crooked below her skirt? Who was it who kept him looking half decent? If it weren't for her mending his socks and cleaning his ties he would go off to church looking like he was dressed for the barn. As it was, he took every opportunity to disgrace her, like the shirt he spilled tea on and then wore in front of everybody.

'She could not go on like this, with never any of her own family to talk to and no friends. If she made a friend who became a true confidante, the other women in the congregation would be jealous. If she made a friend who couldn't hold her tongue, the gossips would have a field day. It was all very well for him to go around visiting and enjoying himself and landing in on people without telling them he was coming and bumming meals off them and expecting her to do the same. That was a habit he got from growing up on the farm where they didn't know their manners. He wasn't always the blessing he presumed he was. She had had it. He was always courting disaster by taking risks and would likely end up hitting his head and dying young like his father and two brothers had. He was driving her to an early grave. And where would he be then if she left him abandoned with three small children? It would just serve him right if she walked out on him.'

The screeching soprano voice reached its crescendo in a desperate cry for help and the tragic heroine collapsed in a heap on the floor. Kathleen Elizabeth Kell had reached the end of her tether. She was going to be heard if it meant yelling at the whole world. She was going to fight to survive and not be crushed under. The light bulb above shuddered in its socket and Mrs. Decoff banged on the other side of the duplex wall to applaud this performance worthy of Sybil Thorndyke in Judith in Israel. In a sudden torrent of tears, Mother picked herself up and fled from the kitchen up to the bedroom where two bear skins lay on the floor, all that remained of a far-off fantasy in the north.

I stayed cowering in the kitchen corner, quaking with fear and pity. I took my cue from Father who was sitting head down at the kitchen table, swiveling his thumb around on his fist, not saying a word except to murmur softly, "Now, now Kay, get a hold of yourself. You are abusing me." I wanted to tell her, "I'm here, Mummy, I'm family" and wondered why Father hadn't gone over and given her a hug, since that was obviously what she wanted. Where was all this *Love* they talked about in this family and in church?

Father knew it was important not to react, not to confront; the pattern of propriety must be preserved. He did not believe in being demonstrative. The example, the pattern of being good people was the important thing, the orientation, the map, the route, the method, the basic attitude, the path God was guiding them in for their lives. Mother's behavior was like a trance, like he had seen an Indian medicine man having. It must be got through, like to a clearing in the bush, to a patch of better behavior and then they would see what they could do. God would help them. If they could not maintain a steady course in their own private lives, how could they continue to set themselves up as role models in the community? In a little while he would go up to the bedroom; maybe she would let him bring her a cup of hot water or a cup of tea. He felt sorry for her. He never should have brought her to this country and into this life that was putting so much stress on her. Perhaps he had strayed in doing so and this was his hell. He must treat her compassionately, as Jesus would have done.

Next morning as we gathered at the breakfast table, my parents were back to normal, although more subdued. The pattern had been preserved at least for now. The example had saved the day. I don't know if her screeching and stomping had loosened it but a few days later the plaster on the ceiling of the upstairs hall and stairwell came thundering down. Two men came in to fix up the mess and we sneezed from the dust for weeks after.

After I dusted off Mother's metal box and opened it in 1996, I found myself reading the diary of a sensitive, delightful seventeen-year-old in her last year at Portsmouth High School. She won the prizes in French, writing and mathematics, was chosen head girl and commended for being responsible. She was on the net ball, lacrosse and field hockey teams and also talented in singing, acting and piano-playing. She got lost in a pea-soup fog on her way to a friend's dance exam in Southampton but used her wits to follow the sound of a car and get directions. She was in love and planning to marry Victor Bracher, brother of her best friend Rene. But then the world fell apart.

Mother, Victor and Rene had been playing tennis in August, 1914, when their game was interrupted by the news that war had broken out on the continent. Earlier that summer, the Prince of Wales had come down to Portsmouth Harbour to review the fleet. The big ships were lit up with colored lights and the townspeople were allowed to ride up close to them in pinnaces. They didn't know the review was really a mobilization and the big ships, one by one, would quietly head up to Scapa Flow afterwards. Now the real thing, an ugly war, was happening. The silhouette of a German Zeppelin airship darkened the Ward bedroom windows. For the first time they sensed danger from the skies. Victor joined up and Mother and Rene went after school to mend clothes and sew on labels at a school turned into a hospital for wounded soldiers. One of the patients shipped home from France suffering from typhoid fever was Victor. He was nineteen years old when he died.

Reeling from this loss, Mother decided to devote her life to helping the sick by becoming a medical doctor. She was accepted at the London School of Medicine for Women but stayed in high school for an extra year, which turned out to be a bad one. She caught the Spanish 'flu, followed by colds, and barely dragged herself to the Armistice celebration on Nov. 11, 1918. Another girl was chosen "most popular" in an open vote and her idol, Lois, didn't write after she left for Oxford. After Lois came back for the Old Girls Dance and asked Mother to two-step, she wrote, "I had never hoped for anything half so nice. I shall now have the occurrence to think about and live over again."

A young man from the Sunday school proposed to Mother but she was not sure she loved him enough to get married. She had five years of heavy studies ahead of her. He was terribly upset when she broke off the affair; neither of them slept for nights. To recuperate, she went to the Lakes district with a friend whose sister was married to a clergyman. But Mother's nerves just got worse. She felt acrophobic while climbing up a slippery mountain. She was horrified when a sudden storm came up and two people drowned in a nearby lake. Then she had to baby-sit with her hosts' toddler and help them pack when they got word they were being moved to another parish. Mother was exhausted when she got back and had to get ready to leave her home and family for the first time in her life.

Her parents and sister accompanied Mother on the train to London and installed her at the home of relatives. When they left, she still had ten days to relax, so they thought, but cousins Norah and Reg suddenly had to have their tonsils out and Auntie Lily came down with an abscessed foot. Mother, who had never even boiled a potato, had to cook for Uncle Frank and run the household. Then, the night before the term started, all England's trains, even London's underground tube, went on strike. Somehow, Walter got a ride from Portsmouth in a saloon car and popped up at the opening guest lecture and sat with Mother.

She loved the campus atmosphere and medical studies; the only problem was the cross-town commute as the strike continued. She had never gotten used to cars and was terrified of traffic. One day, she tried to board a moving bus and would have been dragged under if other passengers had not grabbed her and lifted her up. Another day, she thought she could walk the last part of the way home but got hopelessly lost.

Suddenly, her nerves crocked completely and she could not go on. Walter came to fetch her and she went to see a woman doctor in Portsmouth who prescribed pills and diagnosed her problem as psychasthenia, literally meaning a weakness of the spirit or soul. She had very little nervous stamina and would never be able to lead the life of a doctor. She must take a complete rest and always watch herself to make sure she did not get overtired. Mother faced up to reality and quit medical school. She had hoped to do well and please her parents but didn't want to waste their money.

She soothed her nerves by reading everything from cheap pamphlets on the life of John Wesley to leather-bound works by the Romantic and Victorian poets and novelists. She stared out over the sea from the Isle of Wight, kept a commonplace book of poems and scraps of wisdom, attended church and helped her mother with charitable works. When well enough, she took up dressmaking, needlepoint, cooking, typing and book-keeping at the municipal college. When better yet, she enrolled in a degree program in mathematics, English and history and took part in a suffragette demonstration. After three years of study, she quit just before the final exams after rejecting another suitor.

The J.B. Ward & Sons bakery opened a café above a shop at a downtown intersection around this time and Walter hired his eldest daughter to manage it. This work suited her to a tee. She hired, fired, supervised, ordered food, planned and wrote out menus, served customers, took in cash, kept the books, redistempered the walls and was the gossip center for friends and family.

This was not what she had expected to do with her life, so she busied herself with leading a club for ten-to-twelve-year-old girls from the slums and singing in the philharmonic choir. The lines from the hymn, "Take my lips and let me sing, ever only for my King," inspired her as she sang at benefits. She went out a lot but was too self-effacing by nature to have flair or be able to accept a compliment. She planned to work for Eric, who was setting up a law office and would need help. She did not think she would marry because so few eligible men had survived the war.

Part II

The Exotic Courtship, Marriage,

Honeymoon and Cariole Ride

Norway House Hospital, 1929

6

Why Father Brought Bear Skins Home From Up North

When Mother had her great hysterical fit at Whitmore Avenue and ran upstairs, I thought a bedroom with two bear skins on the floor, complete with heads, eyes, open jaws, teeth and claws, was a strange place to seek comfort. However, my parents had fond memories of the north.

Father had graduated in 1922 with top marks and popularity—his classmates voted him Senior Stick as best pursuer of the motto *The truth shall make you free.* Wanting to begin his ministry the way Jesus had, among fishermen, he took a summer job as student missionary at Warren Landing, a native village at the upper tip of Lake Winnipeg. Now he would discover the reality behind phony summer-camp Indians. A stream of prospectors, trappers, teachers, missionaries, tourists, nurses and administrators came off the steamboat from Selkirk each week and then kept on canoeing north. Father could not resist "the call" and did not return south to enter theology school in the fall as planned.

Instead, he took a job to open a teaching and preaching mission at God's Lake, a community of 328 Swampy Crees located six hundred miles northeast of Winnipeg. One of the aims of the Methodist Church of the time was to evangelize the Indians. Also, the Canadian government wanted to bring the native people, and the Russians (Doukhobors) out west, into a more homogeneous Canada. Education was seen as the key to loosening traditional ties that might foment unrest and threaten the nation's stability. The process would be difficult but Father had faith the natives would choose to progress. He hoped they would follow the white man's virtues, rather than his vices.

After a trip to Winnipeg to purchase a year's supplies, Father went up past Warren Landing to Norway House, the "pantry of the north." It was a trading, manufacturing, tourist, supply, administration and transportation hub inhabited by 700 Indians and 100 white people. The Rev. Samuel "Papa" Gaudin, a most congenial man, greeted Father at the Norway House Mission and would be his supervisor. Samuel and his wife Anna, a nurse, had worked in the north for thirty-six years. Father got instructions and medical supplies from the Norway House doctor, bought a Cree dictionary so he could learn the Indians' language (like the Gaudins had) and then packed his canoe and waited. God's Lake could be reached in six days by those willing and able to portage their belongings twenty times, shoulder their way through narrow bush trails, scramble on hand and knee over high rocks, and slog through foot-deep muskeg (a muddy bog made of decayed vegetation.)

After four days, a war veteran, who introduced himself as John Robertson, and one of his Cree "brothers" came. Soon Father was being guided into the unknown and camping at night with a larger group of Indians who taught him how they worshipped along the trail. They asked Father to lead them in praying and in singing Praise God from Whom All Blessings Flow and other hymns. They paddled for five days across silent, lonely, mirror-like lakes, clear to the bottom, reflecting exquisite northern landscapes and sky.

Then they were dazzled by a spectacularly beautiful display of red, orange and pink sunlight setting on a scene of misery. Five or six houses stood amid rotting trees, abandoned shacks and scores of thin, sniffing, howling dogs. As the canoe approached the lower end of the God's Lake reserve, the people cried out, "The ayumahaogimow (praying boss) is here!" A good man had come to help them gain access to the world of dreams and manitous (gods) and exercise control over the wetigoes (evil spirits) through praying and hymn-singing. Father consulted with the tribal leaders of Weasachewan, held a service and spent the night. They rivaled with the group living at the upper end of the reserve to have him stay and build a church and school here.

The next day, twelve miles farther up at God's Narrows, Father landed in the middle of a large crowd of wedding guests celebrating the Chief's daughter's marriage with drumming, dancing and feasting. The dancers would have gone on all night but the elders quietened them for an outdoor service. Father strung his Navy hammock up in an abandoned summer fish hut, which was offered to him by the departing government officer who also gave Father a list of the indigent families he was to distribute supplies to once a month. While Father waited three weeks for his bags to be dragged in over the swamp by a man who walked all the way from the Echimamish (flowing both ways) River, he observed how the Indians lived.

The Cree were good-looking, jovial, proud, clever people who put out fishing nets that quickly filled with jackfish, whitefish, pickerel, trout and suckers. It wasn't as easy as it looked but Father had to learn how to do it in order to survive. The women snared small animals, like rabbit and mink, while the men hunted big game, like moose, bear, wolf and deer. Father was no weakling but he couldn't match the Indians in speed, strength and endurance. On a twenty-mile run through the bush to see if anyone living in an isolated shack needed help, he came upon Donald Ross who was laid up with sore feet. The only thing Father could think of doing was to soak them in warm water. When Donald recovered, he gave Father some meat and a pair of moccasins so he could run faster.

The Cree resented that the power they had wielded in a Golden Age, when the hunt was plentiful, had been usurped. According to the Government of Canada they were self-governing and self-sufficient but things weren't the same. Father thought it did no good to dwell on what it was like before the white man's arrival. Who would want to go back to the days of no tomahawks, matches, rifles, metal axes, stoves, kettles, pots and pans, embroidery silks, beads and needles? He felt the church and government had behaved generously towards the native people. If they hadn't signed treaties to create reserves with exclusive hunting rights and other provisions, they would have been slaughtered by encroachers or epidemics. But the Cree complained that the white men had misused their women and left them with venereal disease. Tuberculosis and the effects of VD were killing the very young. Eighty-five out of every one hundred people who died on the reserve were under age sixty. Father hoped he could be an example of better behavior on the part of the white man.

He claimed seventy-five acres of land on the other side of the Narrows from the Hudson Bay post and proceeded to erect a log building. He bought an ax, began clearing trees and was startled each time an Indian popped out from nowhere to watch him. When they saw how hard he worked, they volunteered one-by-one to help him. It was already starting to snow as they put moss on the roof, covered it with thin poles and tar paper and got mud to chink the walls by making a bonfire and softening the earth. Then Father banked up the foundation with moss, brush and snow, installed a door, window and stove and built a "parliament building" (Cookstown humor for outhouse.) Dulas McIvor, the HBC factor, gave him old boxes to use for flooring. Dulas was the son of a Scottish trader and a Cree woman. Dulas's wife, Alice, was a graduate of the residential school in Norway House. Her father, a native preacher, had died in the Spanish 'flu epidemic at Cross Lake.

It turned out Father had claimed a holy place, the second highest hill in the whole expanse of land along the old fur trade route from Norway House to York Factory. According to the tribe's ancient beliefs, this hill was inhabited by an otter who was the progenitor of all other otters and had transmitted special healing powers to a medicine man. God's Lake got its name from the abundance of manitous (gods) inhabiting its natural objects, such as a lake teeming with fish and an unusually-shaped rock.

In mid-October, forty-six people in thirteen canoes paddled up for the first indoor church service and one pupil, Job Ougemou, attended the first day of school. Father made the rounds to sell the idea of education. He sat on a box inside the flap-door of Tom Duck's animal-skin teepee and watched fish for winter dog food being smoked on a dozen poles around a fire, which vented itself through a hole at the top. The elders stood on one side and a married son, Elisha Trout, with his wife and children, and the unmarried members of the family on the other. Father knew his sales pitch had succeeded when Donald, Katie and Hattie Trout turned up for school. Soon twelve children were studying the basics of reading, writing and arithmetic. They learned to tell the time, use a calendar and observe a strange custom, Halloween, in which the ayumahaogimow cut his hand when he broke his flashlight while trying to do a shadow trick. After telling the story of Jesus' birth at Christmas, Father went eighty miles by dog team to Oxford House to get presents, ice cream and a Santa Claus suit for a concert. When he returned on a toboggan pulled by a horse (mistatim, meaning big dog) some folks ran and hid. Seventy-five people squeezed into the house for the New Year's Eve watchnight service.

Father was having a dandy time, now that his supplies had arrived and he had learned how to bake bread. He invited the McIvors for dinner several times and they reciprocated. When he shopped at their store for items like chocolate, he picked up the latest gossip: Jimmy, the clerk, had caught an ermine and Alice had received a mink in payment for food. This social life was cut off when Father couldn't get to see them without throwing a rope across the channel, clinging to it as he walked for fifteen feet, then paddling in the canoe, then walking over the ice for another hundred yards. Nothing could get in or out of the reserve as the season changed. Then several dog teams came in from the north and Father was able to mail twenty letters when one of these left for Oxford House. As the temperature plunged, everything else stayed put. Cold, hunger and toothaches set in but were not as hard to bear as the isolation and loneliness of a God's Lake winter.

Father had no radio and seldom anyone to talk to in English. He read novels by Sir Walter Scott and Charles Dickens, jotted down his observations of Cree family structures and social customs, and prepared sermons which Dulas delivered in Cree. One night the Chief came to the door to say that his mother had died. After the funeral, eight dogs pulled her on a cariole (special toboggan) hearse to her resting-place in the cemetery.

On a visit to the Trout/Duck family in their winter shack, Father kicked aside the dozen or so starving dogs and pups in the doorway. Large quarters of frozen moose meat from Lazarus's successful hunt were lying on the roof so now the family and their dogs would be happy. Twelve people lived in the 12' by 15' shack which had no floor, partitions or beds. At night the family slept fanned out on spruce boughs with their feet to the fire and their heads to the outer rim. A huge kettle was boiling on the stove but Father did not accept their invitation to stay for supper. He did not want to run the risk that, in a day or two, they would all be sick by auto-suggestion and blame him for it. Most of the Cree lived in fear of other people's dream gods, thinking they got sick or had bad luck only if someone wanted them to.

While Father was lonely, the natives had Wesukechak, the embittered, flattering one, to keep them company. This hungry wandering superhuman trickster hero of the ancient, oral Cree legends could talk to the birds, animals and spirits—even the Kitche Manitou (Great Spirit.) They knew Wesukechak had never really existed, yet he kept them together. He was just like they were; he was the spirit of the Cree. There was a Wesukechak story to explain everything from how the world was created to why the loon's back was flat. He was tricked, got into fights, got warts on his face and had to solve riddles to find love. The elders embellished the stories as they told them at night around the winter fire. The people kept these intimate, often sexy, myths to themselves because they had been told they were heathen. Father gleaned whatever snippets he could and jotted them down in the margins of his diary (he ran out of paper) because he knew they were more than fairy tales. They were a way of telling a society what it needed to know in order to survive.

On his first solo dog team trip, Father's home-made sleigh fell apart and the dogs ran away so he had to borrow more. He always was more fond of horses than dogs. In February, a guide took him to the Island Lake reserve, a settlement of 625 Indians sixty miles away, to meet the white schoolteacher, Miss Sturdy. As they sped on their way, his guides pointed out Young Lady Lake (three rivals fought for her, two of them killing each other), a split rock (Wesukechak's seat), a spoon-shaped rock (Wesukechak's spoon) and the Lake of Dancing with Your Eyes Shut. At this last spot, Wesukechak tricked all the birds into dancing with their eyes shut and then he ate the duck. Any hopes of a romantic tryst with Miss Sturdy faded when three bachelors accompanied Father to her shack.

When his contract ended in the spring, he reported to the Gaudins in Norway House and fell head over heels in love with their beautiful fifteen-year-old daughter, Esther. It was totally inappropriate for him to have such feelings for his boss's daughter, a mere child who was eleven years younger than he was! He was ready to get married but she had to finish growing up. He couldn't possibly wait for her to become of age. He left the house abruptly, summoning up all the resources he had to resist temptation and not stray from the correct path for his life. He rejected his passion for a woman in favor of his love for Christ. He buried his forbidden love inside him and turned tail. To save his soul and his career, he fled south to the security of Victoria College and an MA program in history.

He wanted to salvage something optimistic from his experience in the north so, before leaving, Father bought two bear skins, one black and one white. He clung to his faith that God would some day provide him with a wife and a home which would be in need of the odd, splendid accoutrement — such as bedside rugs for cold feet.

7

How Mother Beat Father At Tennis and Banished Him

That summer of '37, when we visited Granny's cottage, we were at the spot where our parents played tennis back in '26 after an audacious, transatlantic flirtation. As a child, I wondered about the two tennis racquets hanging like curios in our basement, some joke between my parents. They had a rare laugh when they gave Tanis a small tennis racquet for her birthday and Enid asked if she could have an "Enid racquet" for hers.

Picture my student Father on New Year's Eve 1924/25, standing on the roof of Victoria College to watch the eclipse of the moon. After living in residence for a year, he was boarding in Richmond Hill, once skied into class and sometimes hiked with friends to High Park or City Limits. He was completing the second year of his MA in history under a tutor, "Mike" Pearson, who was Father's age and the son of a Methodist minister. Lester Bowles Pearson was falling in love with a girl in the class, named Maryon Moody, whom he would make the wife of the Prime Minister of Canada almost forty years later.

As Father stood on the roof, he was beginning to savor success. He had a part-time job as a student minister at the three-point charge of Carrville, Headford and Richvale. He had $4,000 from his father's estate and $1,000 from war savings bonds, which he had invested in building lots. He had bought a Ford Touring car for $200 at an auction of bootleggers' cars and not been hurt when the brakes failed on Queen's Park Crescent. The car had hopped the curb and almost slammed into the stone walls of St. Michael's College. All he needed to do now was to complete a year at theological college and get married.

But when he got back down to earth, things didn't go so well. He and his high school sweetheart, Suzy, had grown apart after he came home from the war but it still hurt when she married someone else. He proposed to another girl but she broke off their engagement when she couldn't talk him out of going up north to live on an Indian reserve. He had won the preaching prize at Emmanuel and been offered a job at Metropolitan United Church, one of the city's biggest, so she thought he must be crazy. Father was the best man at two close friends' weddings and wished it would be his turn to be the groom.

On the other side of the ocean in March, 1925, Mother was turning twenty-five and facing spinsterhood. Victor, her first love, had died in the war and all attempts to match her up with someone else had fizzled. She disliked the Varsity snobs she met at tennis parties and dances. In early December, her sister had married an Australian sailor, Joseph Burnett, whose ship was being refitted in the Portsmouth dockyards, and she would follow him to Australia in May. They got back from their honeymoon to find Joe had been put in charge of the crew of twenty-five who would be on duty over Christmas. The question was, how would he round the sailors up and get them back on board after spending their leave wallowing in the debauchery around the harbor? They would all be drunk.

When Elizabeth and Walter got wind of this, they invited the whole crew to come and celebrate Christmas with them. They got all the food ready in Jabez's house, while a party complete with his stories, Eric's conjuring tricks, ukuleles, cocked hats, raunchy Australian songs and recitations rocked their own house next door. Even William Wooller and his maiden daughters had fun. But, at the end of the day, the sailors left and Mother was still alone. Then came May, when her sister sailed away to her new life in Australia.

But the world hath no creativity like that of a woman resisting the fate of spinsterhood and Mother had an idea. In a searching, thorough way she went through the correspondence Enid had been taking care of on behalf of the family and was now abandoning. One of the three Canadian sailors she had been writing to was evidently not married and was enrolled at Victoria College in Canada. Mother had met students from there at an international conference in Swanwick. That's where a speaker on sex impressed her by saying it should be an expression of the entire personality. If she ever found the right man, she would devote herself to him completely, as well as to a higher cause. Nothing in the courtly love convention prevented the lady from lighting a candle to beckon from her tower window and so she sat down in her upstairs office at the café and picked up a pen.

Father was running out of co-eds to date when Mother's letter arrived from out of the blue. How well he remembered Walter Ward's lovely eldest daughter who was not as outgoing as her younger sister. He had surmised that she was already taken. He could not romance her yet, that would not be polite, but Canada and the United Church could.

He replied with knightly courtesy, inquiring if it were not Portsmouth which had the most beautiful women managing its cafés. He admired her business acumen, of which he had none. Theology was his line and he worked on the side as a simple country curate for three small congregations. They were kind folk who teased him about the way he held a baby for baptism. He happened to have a car and would be present at the founding of the United Church of Canada, an event that was attracting international attention.

Ignoring the flirtatiousness, Mother maintained the cover of good family friend, passing on the Wards' news and inquiring about life in Canada. Her family had moved away from New Road, where he had visited them, and were making The Cottage in Waterlooville their permanent home. Soon they would be getting electric light. She enclosed a picture of their grass tennis court and said she was looking forward to playing.

Father replied that baseball was all the rage here but, if he were a decent tennis player, he would offer to play her a game. Since she had asked about life on this side of the ocean, he said the English were behind the Canadians in agricultural methods but not in much else. Some "Old Country misfits" grumbled a lot and the hardier Cookstown villagers felt like telling them to go back home.

The uniting of three of Canada's major Protestant denominations in Mutual Street Arena on June 10, 1925, made one-third of the church-going population of the country into an organic whole. The newspapers of "Toronto the good," "the vestibule of heaven," had run banner headlines of the gathering excitement for a week. Church dignitaries, a crowd of 24,000 in three sittings and a record heat wave combined to make it a heady international event. A wind orchestra played, Communion was served and the Mendelssohn Choir led in singing hymns and the Catholic creed. Just the night before, 8,641 out of 9,433 Methodist, Presbyterian, Congregationalist and Local Union congregations had cast their final ballots to drop their separate names and come together as one. Not since Christians gathered in Nicaea, Turkey, on this same day in 325 AD had such an attempt been made to overcome sectarianism. The United Church of Canada was the culmination of twenty-five years of lobbying and $175,000 spent on legal fees. A feeling of pioneering spiritual adventure surged as it set an example to the world. Tolerance, peace and social justice were envisioned as being just around the corner. Father was in the crowd and wrote to Mother of the "enjoyment, consummation, belonging, spirit, beauty and impressiveness" he felt on this occasion.

The exchange of courteous letters continued until Mother got wound up in the holiday round of work, festivities and balls and let the correspondence lapse. Father waited for the lady to take her turn and, when she finally did, he was not about to let her get away again. He told her he would be one of the first thirteen ministers ordained in the new Church and planned to go north to do Indian mission work for five or six years.

Then his fountain pen splurged out of control and took

on a life of its own, suggesting that she also had a sense of adventure and might want to throw in her lot with his. He said he had always secretly hoped that she, not Enid, would be the one to write and had dropped rather broad hints to that effect. As soon as he mailed this letter, he wanted it back. He wrote again. He hadn't said anything about love because he didn't know whether she was free. He told her he had had a girlfriend at the time he met her, and another one since then, but was now just a carefree youth.

Mother sent back a carefully reasoned answer, feigning surprise. She had always liked him but never thought of him as anything other than a good, close, family friend. However, since they were now writing to each other on this level, it would be best if he could come over for a visit. They had not seen each other for nine years and then only a few times. She was perfectly free, although two men had wanted her but she rejected them. Their letters got through in spite of the general strike of workers in England.

Father could squeeze in a trip to England before his job at Oxford House started and secretly hoped to get engaged now and marry next year. To pay for passage, he sold his car to Wilson and taught him how to drive so he could get back home. Father sent Mother his picture so she would not be expecting to see a twenty-year-old sailor.

Walter met Father in Southampton and brought him to The Cottage, where Mother and Elizabeth were ostensibly relaxing in the garden with a cigarette and a cocktail. Thoughts of the Prohibition petition he had just signed, and all else, fled Father's mind as he looked into the pair of sea-blue eyes he had never forgotten. He was completely overcome by feelings of tenderness, protectiveness and love and was struck dumb. Fortunately, she was a good conversationalist. The girl of his dreams had not changed, even if the school uniform was gone and the long brunette pigtail anchored at the nape of the neck with a huge bow had been replaced by a fashionable flapper's bob.

Mother regretted that he could stay for only six days. They

walked, talked, played tennis, met friends, looked at Eric's law office and saw a play. Walter invited Father to lunch with him and Lord Askwith. He was the guest speaker at a Brotherhood meeting of 1500 men that evening where Father was to read the scripture. This non-church, non-political organization gave homecoming servicemen a place to go to keep up their morale. Organized religion was being rebuffed by postwar society but impulses for human betterment had survived the war. Eventually, the Brotherhood grew to have 13,000 members in forty-two branches spread over several counties.

Mother was finding Father very different from the other young men she knew. The clock was ticking and she had only two days to make the most momentous decision of her life. He could see she was getting tense and felt sorry his presence affected such a dear, intelligent, genuine, sweet creature in this way. On the fourth day, she told him she was very fond of him and enjoyed his company but couldn't possibly marry him. It would be too risky.

That night, the whole household was sleepless. Father felt more miserable than at any other time in his life. Elizabeth found her daughter's behavior reprehensible and felt sorry for him. Mother was a nervous wreck. Walter was convinced his daughter was making a terrible mistake. In the morning, Elizabeth, Eric and Father had an uncomfortable breakfast together. Then he went downtown alone but Walter retrieved him and took him to a Rotary Club dinner at noon.

That evening, Mother came up with an almost giddy idea for a doubles' game of tennis, the men against the women. Walter was an excellent player, capable of secretly throwing a game in order not to embarrass a guest. Father had played only a little in Cookstown and at college. Elizabeth had played all her life. On this occasion Mother was absolutely smashing, her lithe figure bending, stretching and running down every ball. She outmaneuvered even Walter and the women won.

Father's grace at losing was a prelude to his departure, two days later, from the theater of England to begin his lone journey to a mission field five thousand miles away.

8

Kindling a Wee Flame of Love Across Land and Sea

I could not imagine that my parents had ever been attractive or in love; they were just dutifully, decently bound to each other. But I saw them differently after that day in 1996 when I turned the key in the lock of Mother's metal box and let loose seventy-two flimsy, hand-written letters which had logged 200,000 miles between an English city and a Canadian Indian reserve.

The tennis game they played in 1926 was just the opening volley in a lifelong battle of egos and love. Mother was elated by the feminist victory on the court and, the next day, enjoyed touring the Isle of Wight with Father, her mother and her aunt, Alice, in a char-a-banc (a cross between a limousine and a hay wagon.) Father was put back behind the baseline of trusted family friend while the two of them ate lunch in a hotel garden. Mother even told him the blackly humorous riddle which gave the Ward family their identity: The Wards had emigrated from France long ago and set up a farm near Shanklin on the Isle of Wight, where they had twenty-one children twice. (First they had twenty-one but one died. Then they had another one.)

The next day Mother accompanied Father to Southampton, from which he would sail away in the fog and drear. Seized by curiosity, she asked if she could board the SS Minnedosa with him to deposit his luggage and see the inside of a transatlantic liner's cabin. Then they browsed in the dockside shops and bought each other a souvenir. She had to leave first, so he settled her on her train with (I'm willing to bet) a farewell kiss and told her he would not give up hope for a year. She said that if he met someone else in the meantime she would wish them well.

Then she went back to the Isle with a close family circle to rest her nerves for a fortnight. She stared at the sea, took pictures of the lighthouse in the fog and got an awful sunburn.

Father had scarcely set sail when a letter he mailed from Queenstown, Ireland, arrived at Ryde. It was cheery in tone: "I haven't yet met any girl I like better than you," he wrote. "Pardon me for having my little joke but I was really wondering if you thought I could do such a thing. I said "could" not "would." By now, the sight of a lady smoking is no more revolting to me than one chewing gum—they all seem to smoke. But give me good old American spearmint any day." Mother replied that a play she saw made her more strongly inclined than ever to dislike gum-chewing.

Father wrote a diary letter of his ocean-crossing. Among the passengers were several war brides who had been to England to show off their children. The book Mother had given him, Shepherd Easton's Daughter, had led him to ponder a problem at the crux of his ministry. How could one church appeal both to the practically-minded and to the mystically-inclined? The Salvation Army did a good job with the former and the Catholics did a good job with both, at the expense of withholding information and using all sorts of visual symbols. At Quebec City, one hundred steerage passengers disembarked and got on another boat headed for New York City. In Montreal, Father helped some Dutch passengers he'd been tutoring in English find a hotel.

He had to rush on to Richmond Hill to conduct farewell services for his three congregations. Then he visited the farm and sent Mother pictures of Cookstown which, "unlike an English country village, is built around four corners where four main roads meet, each of them going to one of the points of the compass. With regard to buildings, it can hold its own." Now that he knew the person at the other end of the letters, he could make efforts to bond. Mother had hinted at having had a car accident (she had, in fact, demolished the iron entrance gate at St. Cross Hospital in Winchester.) So, when Father disgraced himself by driving Clifton's car right through the garage and six feet out the other side, he told her about it. The gas feed, clutch and brake on a McLaughlin were so different from those on a Ford!

As Father sped westward on the CNR's The National, he had poor substitutes for the wife he had hoped to have with him to share his missionary life. A copy of Gentleman Prefer Blondes lay on his lap and nineteen-year-old (actually seventeen but lying about his age) Jim Johnston sat at his side. The book was from college pals who had sprung a surprise farewell party in Hart House and razzed him about his English girl. Jim was a professor's son who was going up to Oxford House to teach school and would room with Father. Wires laid alongside the railway tracks carried cabled messages and the miracle of radio enabled them to get news "faster than standing-still people." They sat wearing headsets in the lounge car, while a white-gloved operator manipulated the dials to bring in local stations. (This informal network of stations was the forerunner of the Canadian Broadcasting Corporation, which called its newscast "The National" after this train.)

In the dining car, Father sat opposite a Progressive member of the House of Commons who was fresh from the most raucous session of parliament in the country's history. "It proved very exhilarating," Father wrote. "He let out a lot of political secrets and quite convinced me that Premier (William Lyon Mackenzie) King is as crooked as a snake. This customs scandal will come out and turn some Liberals' hair gray. All that talk about Lord Byng's refusing to give dissolution to King and then granting it to Meighen being unconstitutional is a mere cover-up." Late into the night, Father and Jim swayed outside on the dusty caboose.

When they got to Winnipeg, Jim led the search to find just the right radio and, finally, chose one which cost $105, batteries and all. Shopping at a warehouse for a year's supply of food, clothing and other necessities took less time. They bought a tent, blankets, 12 lbs of dried apples, 12 lbs of prunes, 24 cans of peaches, 24 tins of pineapple, 36 lbs of jam, 60 lbs of honey, 100 lbs of bacon and enough baking powder to keep them in bread and cookies. They would barter the jam and honey with the Indians for fish and meat.

Meanwhile, Mother pried open yet-another crate of tomato soup in her café and sat down to take a break. Thinking about what to write to a friend far off in the bush was a creative release. Her day was ten hours long, and often frenetic, but had quiet interludes when she sat in her office or beside the fire. Letters to and from Father had found a niche in her daily round. She felt that his work was important, especially when she read of the loving send-offs his congregations gave him. She needed to let the supportive, frivolous side of her nature come out without making any commitments. One day, she collapsed laughing after a customer said an egg she served him was not as fresh as it might be and a stand-off ensued. Another day, she copied out so many menus she was sure "Tomato Soup" would be found written across her heart when she died. Then she turned serious and wrote, "Isn't it absolutely disgusting that food plays such an important part in people's lives? We are all equally dependent on it but we don't have to be equally fond of it." She recoiled from the over-indulgence she saw at municipal receptions, banquets and balls.

As Mother mused, Father steamed slowly up Lake Winnipeg, checked what time it was on her clock and wrote, "This part of our trip is simply gorgeous with ideal, warm, fresh evenings aboard ship. Canadians, i.e. real born Canadians, are always enthusiastic about our weather. Grumbling at the weather is not the popular pastime here that it seems to be in England." Mother had to agree that if a customer at the cash asked her for the time of day, instead of complaining about the weather, he was making a brilliant effort at conversation.

At Norway House, Father wrote, "The moon is temptingly beautiful, tempting one not to go to bed. You would be agreeably surprised at the community life of this far northern post. There aren't a great many white people but they are of an exceptionally high caliber." Of the residential school graduation exercises for a class of seven, he said, "The boys are eager and the girls well-mannered. The evolution of these people is a fascinating process, full of disappointments and perplexities, but supremely gratifying in the long run."

As he and Jim left Norway House, fifteen new-found friends sang For They Are Jolly Good Fellows and tossed bananas, biscuits and chocolate bars into their canoe. Spruce, tamarack, birch, poplar and jack pine spread a luxuriant carpet over the land as they proceeded past rugged hills and massive rocks displaying early carvings. As they skimmed along, Father wondered how he could help the spiritual growth of the people. "This is a hard job just because so few want to do it or think it worthwhile but I have faith that, being in my right place, my God whom I try to serve will see me through." He feared he was making himself too important, what with being doctor, supplier of government help to the destitute, police magistrate and missionary, but it was all in a lifetime. Isaac Mason (Father's trusted guide from his God's Lake days) traded beans, tea and sugar for freshly killed moose meat when they met a canoe going the opposite way.

After five days of sailing over a multitude of rivers and charming lakes, they reached an ancient summer camping ground of a semi-nomadic tribe of hunters. This gathering-place of the Swampy Cree on the northeastern ridge of Lake Waypinaponipee (water with a deep hole in it) was called Oxford House, less picturesquely, by the white man. From here the Hayes River flowed northeast and emptied into Hudson Bay at York Factory. Father hoped the Chief and his band would interpret the breeze that blew their canoe right up to their feet as a good omen for their mission. Many of them were away working in Norway House as transporters or guides. Father looked down at the rich, black soil at his feet and got his first idea of how he could help these happy, hungry folk.

Inside Mission House, he placed Mother's picture in its Lake Louise souvenir frame on his study desk overlooking a splendid bathing beach. It was July 23, 1926, and this was his birthday celebration. "At last I feel I have stopped running away from you," he wrote.

9

Courting an English Girl While Evangelizing the Swampy Cree

ather's first impression was that some of the people were crude, superstitious and ignorant while others were choice, educated and progressive. One helper, Thomas Noah, was a delightful, remarkable man. He was a leader in the Anglican church at York Factory and preached very well, although Father couldn't understand a word he was saying. He had had one arm shot off at the shoulder but could paddle a canoe, run rapids, drive dog teams, carry freight, trap and hunt as well as any other man. The Chief was also a fine chap who, while not very musical, played the organ and led the singing. Father was amazed at how inspired the people looked when Isaac, an elder, translated his sermons for him. Dulas, who had moved here from God's Lake, understood both languages and told Father the congregation was getting two sermons: his and Isaac's. Some of them understood the humanizing message of a God of love, while others layered it onto their traditional beliefs. It made sense to believe in the white man's god when they were with the white man and in their own gods when they were alone.

Mother wondered how her letter got through to a place with no post office. Father told her it arrived with the treaty party (the doctor and Indian agent) who came by seaplane in early August. He explained that the Canadian government had made the native people its wards at a time (1876) when they were threatened with encroachment and extinction, due to epidemics. Treaties were signed with the main points being:

1) Each band was to surrender its rights to certain lands in return for sole rights to a reserve sized according to a formula of one square mile per man, woman and child

2) Each band was to have free medical attention, a school, a teacher and food for the old and sick. Each family was to be given a quantity of shot, netting, flour, sugar and tea

3) Each band was to receive annuities of $5 for each member, from the eldest to the newest-born. The Chief and Councilors of the native government were to get more.

Mother wrote that she had invited forty little girls from the slums to The Cottage to see a woods for the first time. They yelled, tugged at her skirt and dived heedlessly into the dense thicket to the point where she panicked. With help, she managed to get everybody back together in a "crocodile line." They spent the day having a wildflower-picking contest, playing games and huddling in the diningroom for tea when it rained. Then they climbed onto the char-a-banc to leave, waving and singing Show Me the Way to Go Home. Father said they sang the same song on the reserve but, in contrast to Mother's wards, the Indian girls were shy. They came to his back door with currants and berries but hid around the side of the house until he called "astum" (come here) several times. He served fresh raspberries and red currant pie to his guests, and strained boiled raspberries to make wine for Communion. Among the customers at Mother's café were a teacher who couldn't get a job and a doctor who was working as a waitress. Father said some doctors, dentists and engineers in Canada were having trouble finding work too.

The first month on the reserve, Jim suffered from homesickness and chest pains and was taken out to Norway House. Father had to teach school so asked himself what he would want to learn if he were an ordinary, forward-looking Indian. "I say to myself, if these people had progressed, according to Darwin's principle of evolution, to the place where they would be establishing schools and places of worship, what kind would they be? I think one can sort of graft the principles of Christianity onto their institutions." He found recreation with the children difficult because dance seemed to be their only social tie, apart from the church, and it was hard to regulate. The doctor found out that Jim was only seventeen and told him his problems were due to a drastic change in lifestyle and having grown too fast. He sent him back with the reproof that no one should attempt to live in the north until of military age. School attendance was up from fourteen to twenty-six under Father's program of English, arithmetic, geography, drawing, conversation, calendar, time-telling, singing and group games.

"I walked through the woods to-day and felt absolutely entranced by the superb color combinations in the leaves," he wrote in September. "There has been a breeze off the lake and a little fire in our diningroom has not come amiss. Nature always appeals to me when the wind is bending the trees and white-capped waves roll up on the shore." As winter drew near, he bought Black Beauty, a heifer, from the Hudson's Bay post. She was about to be put down since no one could afford to feed her. He was already looking after Tommy, his predecessor's horse, and could haul enough hay for both animals.

Meanwhile, Mother was pondering whether she could ever leave England or marry a man who wasn't an English gentleman. "Honestly Jack," she wrote, "aren't you proud you're British and of the same race as we?" Then she checked herself and apologized for worshipping the *golden calf* of racism.

The federal election came and went with the reserve four days away from the nearest polling station. Father favored the Conservatives, since they were not tied up to Catholic interests as were the Liberals. He found the Catholics aggressive in trying to make inroads on Protestant territory. Despite the King-Byng Affair, the Liberals got back in.

It snowed fiercely as the Cree moved out to their winter camps in groups of four or five families. They would live in shacks, shoot ducks and moose, and fish for themselves and their dogs. The children would be more contented and healthy out in the bush with meat to eat. Father and Jim gave them their scribblers and texts and told their fathers to make sure they spent some time at them each day. The elderly, the mothers with small children, and men who were too sick or injured to hunt stayed behind.

Father was finding it was no mean trick to keep a transatlantic courtship going. An old man who was bringing the freight in from Norway House took sick and left his bundle of supplies and mail destined for Oxford House tied to a tree ninety miles away. Father sent two men after it. A float-plane dropped down but didn't stay long enough to pick up a letter. After that, Father resolved always to have one partially written. On October 10th, he was writing about his potato crop when he heard a plane. He rushed out, stuffing the letter inside his waistcoat from whence it disappeared in the snow. Fortunately, the plane contained three map-survey photographers who wanted to stay overnight so he had time to write another one. They were getting set to leave when he realized this was his chance to send Christmas greetings to the Wards. He had bought Mother a pair of embroidered white deerskin fur-trimmed moccasins made for an Indian princess. As he was running to the plane, he saw the letter he had lost in the snow so sent it too.

Mother kept on writing regularly, even if she got no replies. She thought Father was a real sport for doing what he was doing and wished they could sit down together and have a good old chat. She was reading H.G. Wells's The World of William Clissold, while he was reading books on the North American Indian. He believed in offering the people constructive ideas without scolding—one of the worst crimes people commit, he felt, well deserving of punishment under the law. Mother pleaded "Guilty" and wondered what her sentence should be.

The reserve's only radio picked up concerts each night from New York, Chicago, San Antonio, Los Angeles, Washington, Portland and Seattle. The Zion Broadcasting Station, built and financed by a very religious man in Illinois, was one of the strongest in America and sent out nightly concerts which came in very distinctly. After seeing a snapshot of Father, Jim and the

Hudson Bay folk sitting spellbound, Mother wrote, "You seem to have rapt expressions which might, I suppose, be called radio face." One night Father was up late, waiting for the bread to bake, when he heard a tenor voice singing Do I Miss You? Deed'n I Do. He wrote, "It's lonesome up here and I'm thinking always of you, wanting you for my companion and inspiration. I would be raised to seventh heavens of joy if you would give me your love. Somehow I feel absolutely safe with you; I never felt the same with anyone else. I feel no barrier whatsoever. All that I have is yours. I know not if this is not for some purpose which lies beyond our ken. I wish we could tune in to one another's thoughts." Silence from Portsmouth.

An urgent knock on the door summoned Father to go out to the Chief's winter camp. He had gone crazy and was terrorizing the people. After getting there as quickly as possible, Father calmed the Chief down and held a service with the people. On the trip home, Father and his guide, Jamesie Robinson, came upon a burly wolf who had two toes caught in a trap and was fighting to get free. Jamesie said they must kill the animal before it chewed off its foot and got loose. They picked up two sticks and administered six swift blows to the animal's head until it fell down dead. They left the carcass slightly covered with snow so the owner of the trap would be able to claim his pelt.

Mother's letters were piling up in Norway House with no one wanting to go for them, so Father got an idea. He knew his beloved Tommy, a small, efficient, intelligent animal, was capable of making the trip. In early December, he hitched him up to a toboggan and set out with Robert Chubb as his guide.

Fortune smiled on the arduous 180-mile trip over snow and ice. On the way, an Indian couple asked Father to baptize their baby son, Evangeline. In Norway House, the Gaudins were in bed sick so Father preached for them. His feet were sore from trekking in a pair of ill-fitting boots, which the school principal noticed and so sold him his own pair cheaply. Then the Hudson Bay factor gave him a deal on a new toboggan. The twenty-seven pieces of mail Father picked up included several from members of his former congregations. In a Sunday School "budget letter" of dozens in one envelope, a girl inquired if the boys on the reserve were good-looking. A mother of three boys thanked him for having saved her marriage. All Father wanted from life was to help somebody and be a true friend but he found it difficult to assess whether he was doing any good. When Mother read all this she wrote, "I think you've found the biggest secret of how to make life happy for yourself and others. It makes me look around and see if there's not somebody I can help a little more. That really is practical Christianity, isn't it?"

Saving the best for the last, Father put the six letters Mother wrote between October 14th and November 10th in chronological order and sat on his free cot in the residential school reading and re-reading them, pretending to be living with her. She said his account of how he canoed to a prospector's camp at Knee Lake in September, and carried a detonator in one hand and 75 lbs of dynamite sticks in the other over a portage, read like a novel. Only it was better because it was real life. She could picture him eating sourdough bread around a camp-fire outside a lean-to, going with his guide to shoot a duck for supper, panning for gold and staking a claim. In that letter Father had said he was greedy for love and wanted to have her with him all the time. No comment on that.

He loved Mother's scoop on the Prince of Wales's visit to receive the key to Portsmouth: "My parents went to the Presentation of the Freedom Ceremony in the Guildhall when a rather amusing incident occurred. I think you heard, when you were here, what kind of a man our Mayor Privett is — a great lover of ceremony and etiquette and very hopeful that this visit of the Prince will bring him a knighthood or even a baronetcy. Well, the ceremony proceeded as it should until the moment came for the Town Clerk to step forward with a book for the Prince to sign. He placed it on the table in front of him and the Mayor pulled from his pocket a beautiful silver pen with a new nib (no doubt destined to be handed down as an heirloom to future generations of Privetts as the pen with which the Prince of Wales signed when he was presented with the Freedom of the City, etc. etc. etc.) and handed it to the Prince.

"But, behold, there was no ink. The Mayor scowled, the Town Clerk hastened to ask the reporters for some—but there was none. Then Alderman Foster, who hopes to get a knighthood before the Mayor and between whom and the Mayor there is little love lost, quietly got up and handed the Prince his fountain pen. Somebody in the Town Hall will suffer because of the missing (l)ink."

Before he left for Oxford House, Father cabled greetings to the Ward family to be delivered on Christmas Day. By the time he made it home through a snowstorm with two toboggans loaded with presents and food, he had never in all his life been so happy to see a couch and a radio. Tommy had made the first round trip by horse from Oxford House to Norway House and he had cut two days off the time it would have taken any dog team.

Mother's "too great a whirl of gaiety for such a sober-minded individual" included amateur Shakespearean productions and professional London revues trying out in Portsmouth. She transformed the Portsea girls into white angels for their Christmas concert, sang in the philharmonic society's production of Faust and enjoyed games at friends' house parties. By day, she was "glued to the café," her fingers in a perpetual state of stickiness from putting cakes out on plates. The slippers that arrived in a slipshod parcel from the Oxford House mission elated her and the cable from Canada added fizz to an otherwise flat Christmas Day. She sent Father one of each special Christmas magazine issue the bookstore sold.

As for the Mayor's Ball on New Year's Eve, "About twelve hundred guests were present so you may guess what a brilliant assembly it was, what with the pretty decorations, the ladies' frocks and the bright uniforms of military and naval men. To my great surprise (this is a little bit of swank) my frock was very much admired—one lady said she thought it was the most striking one there. I'm sure that was quite an accident; I've never set out to achieve that kind of notoriety. But I'm glad people liked it." Father's New Year's, called ochama kesagow (kissing day), was anything but brilliant. He spent it lost in a maze of lakes and bushes on the way into God's Lake with his old guide, William Grieves, who was half blind.

Being non Indian, Father and Tommy had to go off the reserve to haul wood. It was a lot quicker and cheaper than hiring a York boat and six men to bring wood in the summer time. He could get as much as he wanted for $35 a season, the cost of hiring men to cut it. In contrast, Jim's parents' fuel bill for their house in Toronto was $175. Even when the thermometer said -12 degrees, the cattle were still out pasturing and Father was wearing light clothing. He wrote, "We suffer little or nothing from the cold up here, although our friends down east think we must almost perish." When the temperature settled at -49 degrees, however, he opted for staying inside to "read, read, read and look at seed catalogues." In mid-February the bright moon and sun alternated so the sky was never left untended.

Two of Father's theology pals disappointed him by dropping out of Indian mission work after trying it for less than a year. He wrote, "All mission work looks romantic and appealing at first but on the field of action it is full of drudgery and disappointment. Still, I love these northern skies, the stars, the frosty air, the cheery fire and these dark-skinned, primitive folk. They are so tantalizing and yet so much in need of a bit of intelligent, patient interest. It is neither promising nor charming but that is precisely why I want to stick with it. If I carry out a third of my dreams no one will say I have thrown my life away or buried it in the bush." A blizzard of snow did almost bury him when he went to Bear Crossing Lake in mid-March to bring a fifteen-year-old, Alfie Jowsie, in for school until his trapper parents could pick him up in the spring.

Soon the sun would begin to melt the four feet of snow lying like lead over Oxford Lake but now nothing stirred for a month. Alfie became so attached to Jim he stayed up looking out the window for him if he went out at night. Then a splendid mail arrived containing all the British Christmas magazines and a book. In all, Father got seventy letters full of good news. These were the optimistic twenties — taxes were going down, farm values were rising, his salary was going up, etc., etc.

10

Waiting For the Spring Thaw, Dying For a Reply

A whiff of spring in England put Mother in a mood to visit the babies at the unwed mothers' home, where she was a volunteer, and to think about tennis. She had never quit crowing over last summer's victory when she and Elizabeth had beaten Father and Walter. She asked Father how the United Church of Canada observed Lent and how its order of service differed from the Anglican one. She took the Portsea girls to see a missionary exhibit at the Guildhall, not just once but twice, and asked Father questions about Oxford House in winter. Her interest in these topics gave him hope.

On April 9, 1927, the last dog team of the season left Oxford House over the ice for Norway House bearing an urgent letter. By the time it arrived in Portsmouth, the year of not-giving-up-hope which a suitor had been promised would be almost expired:

"My Dear Kathleen,

"I have been trying hard to rethink the entire situation as it exists between you and me. Sometimes I think how foolish I have been to even think of you as anything but a friend, first because I'm too ordinary a fellow and second because I'm in very unattractive work. And then something happens to make me feel better. I say to myself I won't always be living away back here and my hopes are rekindled.

"Does everyone pass through such periods of

discouragement and encouragement, I wonder? They come to me as regularly as the moons but somehow I always manage to come out on top so I don't worry too much about them. Sometimes I think I am a somebody and other times I'm only Farmer John with his overalls on. When I am in the former mood I sing Nobody But You Dear, Nobody But You and when in the latter mood I don't sing at all. I just saw wood.

"I hope you don't mind my pulling the curtains back and letting you have a glimpse of my inmost reflections. I feel very priggish writing to you as I have been doing all the time, wondering whether you like me or not. Tell me, won't you Kathleen, whether you like me well enough to give me a chance to win you. I will look forward with life and death interest to your answer when the first canoe arrives.

"With love, Jack."

The interlude of waiting for a reply drew on as Father hauled wood. One of the worst snowstorms of the year created eight foot drifts on April 20th. But, by June, the people of Oxford House were basking in California-like sunshine and had forgotten all that. The first canoe, on June 16th, brought six letters from Mother, obviously written before she got his crucial one. She wrote that at the annual meeting of the sponsors of her favorite charities she had an impulse to screw up her treasurer's report and throw it at the audience. "So much for me and public speaking." She had been to see The Wooing of Katherine Parr and discovered she was a very romantic person underneath her cold exterior. (Then she added, "Dear me, what am I saying?")

Meanwhile, Tommy balked at having to haul manure for the gardens Father had planted. The seeds sprouted quickly in the long days, when the evening glow never really disappeared. It only shifted to the north and east to become the morning glow. Jim left at the end of school but Alfie and two trappers remained in Mission House. Five prospectors arrived and two mining experts came up to verify last year's gold find at Knee Lake. Father put his guests to work washing dishes, carrying water and helping prepare meals. Often visitors to the reserves undermined the native's confidence in the white man, so he insisted that anyone who stayed with him act decently and attend church. The prospectors were not rough and uncouth, as one might assume. They were well-read, widely-traveled men who jumped with ease from Africa to Alaska in conversation. They gave Father a concoction of citronella, camphor, carbolic acid and castor oil to fight off mosquitoes.

Father had to force himself to deal with the pile of letters from Mother which did not contain her answer to his heartfelt plea. He tried to sympathize with her efforts to entertain the French fleet at a ball held in their honor. When she said, "I am not a social butterfly; I really prefer the simple life," he replied, "That's what we have up here all right" and enclosed a picture of his house with the outhouse some distance away. In answer to her questions about winter, he said the people wore woolen clothes, not furs. He had a water-hole in the lake, which he kept open by using an ice-chisel, and at sunset he drove Blackie and Tommy down for a drink. Then he filled two pails of water and carried them up to the house on a home-made yoke. Just now, three men were working in his gardens and the oats, buckwheat, millet, turnips, carrots, peas, beans, parsnips, tomatoes, radishes, cauliflower and cabbage were already up. To follow were Sudan grass, potatoes, lettuce, beets, sunflowers and corn. He had planted a dozen different kinds of flowers and was waiting to see what they were.

As he was writing on June 26th, a letter was brought to the door and Father tore it open. Then he dropped it to the floor in despair. He had to write again:

"Kathleen my dear,

"The mail has just arrived and I have before me your letter of June 2nd in which you remarked that you had not heard from me for six weeks. If that's the case, a letter from me, a most important one, has gone astray. It left here on April 9th and should have reached you about the middle of May at the latest.

It makes me sick to think we can't trust even the poor mail service we do have.

"In that letter I told you a whole lot of things about myself, among them being the longing in my heart to have your companionship through life. I think of you continuously and when at my best I feel that I can't get along without you. Sometimes I feel that, in all fairness to you, I should not ask you to share life with me. But most of the time the future seems rosy and I feel confident I could make you happy. As the days come and go I seem to want you more and more. I know you are giving me every consideration you possibly can and I know too that you will have to love me a great deal because, in the eyes of the world at least, I have not a great deal to offer you. One thing I feel proud of is that I have a group of friends who are the very finest folk in the world. As far as living up here is concerned, from the point of view of experience it is most desirable. The cold is not a factor to be feared for wood is cheap and it is not difficult to keep the house warm. The isolation is the biggest drawback but if I had only you to be my companion and helpmate I would not mind that in the least.

"But, while I tell you all this, I know that the outward aspects of our life together would neither attract nor detract you i.e. in any deciding way. It is because I love you on account of your mind and character—but also, I must admit, because of your charming appearance—that I would dare to ask you to be my wife. Your letter received today is a real disappointment but the delay will be forgotten a hundred times if your answer now is favorable.

"With love, Jack."

The next day an unexpected canoe paddled in and this time there was no mistaking the pretty, lavender paper postmarked Portsmouth. The letter containing Father's earnest plea for Mother's love had dallied transatlantically for eight weeks but, when it finally arrived, she had acted swiftly to relieve his agony:

"My Dear Jack,

"I am very glad you have asked, Jack, because ever since you left here last year I have been in a very unsettled frame of mind and cannot even now say where I stand. However, I feel I owe it to you to tell you, as far as possible, some of the moods and thoughts to which I have been subject. I leave it to you to draw your own conclusions and act accordingly. First of all, I am quite certain that when I said "No" last June I was doing the right thing. However much my mind may have urged me to say "Yes," deep down I had a feeling I simply could not. You were not prepared to accept that answer as final and I felt, as you wanted me so badly, I could do nothing else but go back and think the whole matter out again.

"At times I was, and still am, seized by attacks of pure funk. I think how very little I know you and have seen you, and imagine all the terrible things that might happen if we married and were not happy. And then I think what a fool I am, and realize that I am not of a nature to be violently or passionately in love. For me a marriage based on deep, trusting friendship would be ideal and the only one possible. And I do believe, Jack, that you and I have similar tastes and would get along well together.

"I have prayed a lot and refuse to lose my faith that whatever we decide will be for the best. And that brings me to what I believe will be the best course of action. If you really think it worth your while I would like you to come over again when you can be spared for a few weeks from your work. I think there is a sporting chance that I may throw in my lot with yours. You have never been long out of my thoughts during the last year and many times I have badly wanted to see you.

"On the other hand, Jack, I want you to face the fact that I may know quite definitely and finally that I do not want to marry you. There are times when I feel that the last thing I want to do is to marry you, or for that matter, any man. But I think if we could meet again we could quite definitely find where we stand and decide our future relations. I am very ashamed I do not know my own mind better and have not liked writing this letter. Put so badly, one's thoughts take on an unpleasant and distasteful aspect. But I think you will understand and I want you to know what I feel and think. Now, I am perfectly aware that you may dislike me, upon discovering the state of my mind, and think me a most objectionable little prig. Or, you may not be prepared to make another trip to England. But if you still do want me very badly, Jack, and think it worth your while, I shall be very pleased to see you.

"In any case, I want you to do just what you like—don't hurry to decide, but really think what will be the best. I shall understand and not be hurt because, above everything, I want to make you happy. Do not, by the way, worry about your work. I am quite prepared to share it with you wherever it may be. And if I do decide to marry you I will not keep you waiting long.

"Kathleen."

Father did not hesitate to reply:

"June 27, 1927

"My Dear Kathleen:

"I do appreciate the spirit of frankness you show in your letter and think I can, to some extent at least, understand your feelings. We have not seen much of each other, it is true, and yet I seem to know what you are doing all the time. You can't say that of me because I don't write such good letters as you do. But I think I will be able to go over and see you in October. I have been counting on going as far as Winnipeg at that time and can arrange to go on, coming back here about December 15th so as to help the teacher prepare for the Christmas entertainment. While my feelings will be those of a gambler making his last throw, I am greatly encouraged when you say there is a sporting chance you may cast your lot with mine.

"I too have prayed about this matter a great deal and must

confess I have been selfish and at times rather insistent—like *the importunate widow*. I know it is possible to imagine all sorts of calamities that might befall us but doesn't every young couple face the same possibility? And why should we look for the ill rather than the good? None of the evil things I have feared the most have ever happened and I strongly doubt they will provided my attitude to life is the correct one.

"I am so glad you added those remarks about my work. If there is one thing that is dearer to me than anything else in the world it is my profession and, perhaps I should add, my citizenship. I am proud to be a Christian minister and proud to be a Canadian citizen. No other work appeals to me like this work yet I am fully aware it has no monopoly on Christian service. You are just great to say what you do about being ready to share my work in such a whole-hearted manner—if the major question is once settled. Well, we will talk about all that if I can possibly manage to go over in October. In the meantime we will be just the same real friends that we have been all along.

"With love, Jack."

II

Father Leaves the Bush, To Gamble On a Sporting Chance

Charles Lindbergh was guest of honor on Parliament Hill for Canada's sixtieth birthday while, up at Oxford House, Father shared his first radishes with his men and gave them the day off from building a fence. He looked forward to the time when these wards of the Government of Canada would be full citizens of the country. On Jubilee Sunday, a Day of National Thanksgiving, the whole nation tuned into a simultaneous broadcast with the order of service written by federal MPs. To Father this was a historic step towards becoming a Christian commonwealth. He told the natives "Canada" was an Indian word and "dominion" was taken from the Bible. The Jews had a vision of what God expected of them and, in the same way, Canadians were chosen to show how a nation may be built in peace, righteousness and sincerity, and how people of varying religions and races may live together in one nation with tolerance and honor. His dinner guest was the guide who had led the Duke of Connaught from Norway House to York Factory years ago.

After singing The Fairy Laundry at a rainy garden party to raise money for the unwed mothers, Mother wrote Father an especially nice letter on his 30th birthday:

"My Dear Jack,

"I am most awfully glad that you think you will be able to

come over in October and I hope with all my heart that I shall be able to give you an answer that will make you happy. But you understand, don't you—there is a factor in my make-up that I am not sure of and that made me feel as I did last year. I am hoping that when we meet again all my doubts and fears will disappear. Nothing would make Mummy and Daddy and the rest of the family happier than for you to be added to it—they have told me so.

"One other thing I want to say to you. You make me feel very humble when you pay such attributes to my mind and character as you did in your last two letters. I am not anywhere nearly like the wonderful person you imagine—please do modify your ideas a little or you are going to be very disappointed when we meet. I am very, very ordinary and not the least worthy of you. There, I have unburdened my mind and so will close, knowing that at any rate for the immediate future we are still the good friends we have always been.

"Yours affectionately, Kathleen."

This was Mother's ego laid bare. It really was not very big but she staunchly supported it. When Father got this letter he went out for a walk in the starlight. Imagine that the Wards would welcome him into their family! He had feared that they mightn't, since Enid had moved so far away—but the world was getting smaller. He felt sorry for having put Mother in such a difficult position. Permeating his thoughts of her was a deep feeling of mystery and wonder. He visualized the two of them together, "High, high up in the sky, watching the world go by." The only direction in which he could revise his estimate of her was upwards. But he mustn't anticipate too much. At any rate they would be the best of friends. After coming home from trying to settle a quarrel between a husband, wife and mother-in-law, he pressed some garden flowers and enclosed them in a letter.

Mother's cousin, nineteen-year-old Jack Bernard Ward, was bent on joining the police force in India but the family persuaded him to go to Canada, where agricultural help was badly needed. After an exchange of letters instigated by Walter, Clifton invited Bernard to work on the Kell farms at Cookstown. He was a tall, conscientious boy who excelled at horse-riding, marksmanship and swimming. Father told Mother that Mary Jane would be a kind, intelligent friend but she was Irish and expected people to "step around." Mabel would do all she could to make things comfortable. His brothers worked so fast no one could possibly keep up with them. Things were done in a more haphazard way than on an English farm but the output was greater. The young people were jovial because they were constantly being told this was their country and they could make it into whatever they wanted it to be. Father was sure Bernard was "the right sort" and, from his first letters home after arriving, this appeared to be true. He said the family was wonderful, he was enjoying himself and the farm was one of the finest in Canada.

Mother's café did brisk business when Princess Mary passed along the street three times within one hour. Father sent her a diary letter starting with a wedding write-up:

"Monday: I was putting rolls of wire on the fence around 4:15 p.m. when young Edwin came up and said "They're ready." "Who's ready?" I asked. "The wedding" he replied. Sure enough, a hundred or more people were streaming down the road towards the church. Well, I thought to myself, if they can't give me more warning than that they will just have to wait. "You tell them I'll be ready at six o'clock," I said. Edwin went away but then the Chief came and said he had sent a boy to tell me but he must have forgotten. I took this as a bona fide excuse and went in to get changed. Usually I wear a white bow tie and wing collar but the shirt with the tie buttons was dirty so I wore a wedding-gray tie. The bride wore a white dress made out of muslin purchased at the Hudson Bay store three hours before. We got through the ceremony with Edwin translating. I took pictures on the church step and all was over by 6 p.m.

"Tuesday: The verandah was particularly breezy and inviting so I put up an awning to shelter the hammock from the sun and read Clark Wissler's The American Indian. After supper a canoe-load of medical supplies arrived from Winnipeg and I repacked and sent on those destined for God's Lake. Then I baptized a baby at his home.

"Wednesday: I began to unpack and stow away a thousand pounds of medicines, including eighteen gallons of cod liver oil. The freight I ordered didn't arrive because I had forgotten to sign my check. A little three-year-old girl is suffering from some kind of brain or nervous trouble so I mixed a bottleful of sodium bromide and took it over to her. Then I called on a fourteen-year-old girl who is suffering from TB and gave her a bottle of cod liver oil. I always let the people try their own remedies first and only give them white man's medicine if they ask for it. Two little boys are suffering from the severest form of TB which has symptoms similar to spinal meningitis and I had to tell their parents I can do nothing for them. Many of the people have bigger families than they can care for and TB captures the weak, sickly ones.

"Thursday: I gave the Chief paint for the inside of the school and walked over to see how the men were doing. They didn't know they should take the pictures and blackboard off the wall so I did, and I explained that they shouldn't paint the windows. After the evening prayer meeting, I settled into my hammock to read a book on law until it got dark at 10 p.m. A canoe with an engine arrived with mail from Norway House after only two and one-half days!

"Wednesday: Dr. Grant, Professor of Anatomy at the University of Manitoba, is here with two men and a box of instruments. He is measuring these people—their height, stretch, cranium, mouth, nose etc.—what for, I do not know. On Sunday he spoke in church and said the doctors are hoping to be able to use these measurements to forecast which diseases an individual is most likely to contract. He is an Old Country man of the "oh-rather" type, but not a bad sort.

"Saturday: Mr. Barner, the superintendent of Indian missions, arrived before Dr. Grant's canoe was out of sight. He is the most delightful of superintendents, never criticizing but always inspiring. I told him about you and he was glad to hear of my plans. He doesn't think I'm gadding about too much and will try to help me get a special-rate train ticket.

"Monday: At a meeting yesterday the men were given a chance to ask questions or make suggestions and one man told Mr. Barner how much they like me. Such an expression of appreciation is apparently rare. He is now putting on my bathing suit for a run into the lake before we go visiting. Tomorrow there will be three services and an ordination of two elders. I asked Mr. Barner about getting a furnace and he was quite in favor so I will get that work done next summer. A few of the men are watching him very carefully as he splashes around in the lake. These people do not take advantage of their beautiful, clean lakes and rivers for bathing purposes because they suspect that going into the water makes them weak. One old man told me he takes two baths a year: one when he tips his canoe and the other when he falls through the ice."

In August, Father had more anecdotes to tell about his work:

"The airplane with the treaty party did not arrive so for four days we scanned the clouds and strained our ears. Then, in the middle of the church service, I noticed an unusual amount of whispering in the congregation, "chemanuk, chemanuk," and found that two canoes had come in. One had a flag flying."

"I invited four Americans passing through on their way to York Factory for tea. They were impressed with our people and my garden and say I have better potatoes than in Cincinnati. They asked Dulas many questions, which he answered patiently, about the Indians, their language and his wife. Alice served tea and they couldn't believe she is pure Cree, at least as pure as any people can be after six generations of association with white people."

"Some men who were cutting hay have returned to say they have put up five tons. It's a pleasure to find men who can be trusted to do such work. Next we'll build a stable."

"For ten years this school has been conducted with a home-made table and benches and this afternoon I nailed four boards on top of boxes. Some table! I have spoken to the Indian agent and he has promised to do his best to supply proper seats and desks."

"My associations with these people are extremely happy, except that they do have a faculty for tiring one and doing disappointing things. When one wants to speed up the rate of progress one feels the burden heavily. But if one doesn't feel that way at times the consequence is laziness and apathy—a state of affairs I dread."

Father was glad when Mother confided in him. The week of the August Bank Holiday her family deserted her to go on vacation, leaving her feeling lonely and rotten. On top of coping with an extra crowd of customers, she had to fire her kitchen maid at the café. Her work had been unsatisfactory for some time, but the last straw was when she refused to wipe the brass rods that kept the stair carpeting in place. After Mother's family got back, she went to Winchester with her aunt and uncle, the Warmans, and a friend of theirs, to tour the Church and Hospital of St. Cross (which had a new gate.) They drove off with Uncle at the wheel and Mother beside him and were going along nicely when a car veered out to pass a truck and came straight at them. Mother was sure she was going to die! At the last split-second the hysterical driver squeezed in between them and the truck and got back on her own side of the road. The truckdriver cursed, Uncle turned apoplectic, and Auntie and her friend screamed. Mother, however, did not experience the least fear or thrill. Her famously lousy nerves were shock-proof in a real emergency!

Amid an abundance of sweet peas, phlox, cosmos, marigolds, poppies and pansies, Father basked in the perfect days and balmy nights of early September. Then he stopped dreaming and got started on an important project—a new winter trail. He wanted to link Oxford House up with the new Hudson Bay Company (HBC) line at Mile 214 or Pikwitonei (sore mouth) one hundred and forty miles distant. If he succeeded, it would mean a tremendous lot to the natives, since another group of traders would be able to come in. When he first came north, he thought the HBC was a benefactor to the people. But now he saw it as getting a poor, ignorant Indian into a corner, extracting his fur for the lowest market price and charging him the sky for his food.

Father had discussed the matter of the trail with the district manager of the HBC and, when he saw how emphatically opposed he was, he decided he absolutely must go ahead. The trail would be mostly over lake-ice with only about twenty miles of bush to be cut through. He would hire natives who knew the territory to do the work in sections. Even if it cost him $200, it would be worthwhile. The first day Father and two men working for the whole day were only able to cut through about one mile of bush. It was very slow going but the men would continue working while he was away.

A tennis partner arrived just in time to help Father practise his game, which was atrocious except for the odd, spectacular ace. Nelson Gaudin, the missionaries' son and brother of Esther, was replacing Jim Johnston as schoolteacher and room-mate. He was more fluent than Father in Cree, so more Indians dropped into Mission House to talk freely and verbosely.

Father wanted to take off in mid-September and be in Toronto in time to attend centenary celebrations at the university but someone broke into Dulas's store. The RCMP arrived, a rowdy council meeting was held and Father waited for the hullabaloo to settle down. He was walking a cow on a leash when she bolted, dragging him into the bush and whipping off his glasses so he couldn't find them. He couldn't read without his eyes getting sore. Then a vicious head-wind came up, locking in his canoe.

While Father waited to get going, he dreamt up an amusing sermon. He pretended otherwise but it was really just for himself and Mother. This was "their" sermon. The text, *Put out thy hand and take it by the tail,* depicts the Lord placing a serpent before Moses and telling him to pick it up. The points it illustrates are (1) Do not be afraid to attempt the hard task (2) There is a safe way to begin, and (3) The Lord will never ask anyone to do anything which is not feasible. When Moses reached down and picked up the serpent, it became a staff, a symbol that the hardest task by an almost-magical process becomes our main source of support. "I don't, of course, accept this story as actual history but it sparkles with interest all the same," Father wrote. Finally he shoved off on September 28th, leaving Isaac and Nelson in charge of the mission.

12

A Fairy-Tale Marriage
Gets Off To a Rickety Start

When Father got to Winnipeg, he bought a train ticket to Toronto and was glad to have 67 cents left over. After the overnight trip, he went straight to Burwash Hall, the men's residence at Victoria College, and had a bath, shave and breakfast. He withdrew $100 from his bank account on Yonge St., had his hair cut and bought a suit, shoes, shirt, gloves and hat. Then he visited the dentist, who extracted nine rotted teeth and fitted him for a temporary plate to be picked up the next day. That done, Father bought a new pair of glasses at the optician's and hopped on a bus for a quick trip to Cookstown to visit his family and share his news. His comings and goings made an interesting gossip item for the social columnist of the local weekly newspaper and Wilson paid him $500 for past work on the farm. Back in Toronto, Father bought a boat ticket to England and boarded the overnight train for Ottawa. He had breakfast with his sister, Clara, in the new Chateau Laurier Hotel before buying a passport and continuing on to Montreal.

Father embarked on the Ascania on October 14th, clutching a fox fur he had bought for $50 at the railway station. Ernie Taylor, who was now with the Montreal YMCA, his wife Mary and their two children waved him on. When the boat reached Quebec City, Father sent a cable to Portsmouth to give the Wards his estimated time of arrival ten days hence.

Then Cinder Jack settled down in a deck chair with a book and didn't notice his fairy godmother smiling down on the bumpkin transformed into Prince Charming.

When Mother looked into Father's eyes at Cosham railway station in Southampton, all her fears and doubts fell away. She was positive that everything was going to be all right. However, to make sure her misgivings were gone for good, she decided to watch over her emotions for three days and four nights to see if any bad feelings returned. On October 27th, as she and Father waited to catch a bus to London to have lunch with friends, she told him she was going to marry him. They picked out a diamond ring at a jewelry shop in Trafalgar Square and that night there was great rejoicing in The Cottage.

Elizabeth had little time to plan a wedding, since Father had to sail away on November 5th, but she phoned as many relatives and close friends as possible. Everyone pitched in. The maid cleaned Father's clerical collar with a bread crust since they couldn't find a supplier of new ones. The bishop in charge of the local Anglican parish of St. George granted a quick marriage licence after Mother signed an affidavit swearing that she resided in Waterlooville. The night before the wedding, Walter drew Father aside and honorably warned him, "She has a terrible temper."

My parents said their vows on the rainy morning of Nov. 2, 1927, plighting their "troth" and promising "to love and honor thee only, forsaking all others, till death us do part." The only picture of the bride in a navy blue suit wearing a hat and fox fur is blurry. They left their guests to linger at The Cottage over coffee and cake while they caught the noon luncheon train to London. That night they slept in the honeymoon suite of the Hotel Belgravia.

Early next morning, Mother and Father soared off on their married adventures in Imperial Airway's twelve-passenger, deluxe Silver Wing flying out of Croydon Airport. It was a four-hour leap over the English Channel. Mother's aunt, Clara, her uncle, Jim, and cousins Joan, Lois and Norah, watched them taxi down the grass; there was no runway. The canvas of the airplane was so thin that Jim remarked he could have poked his finger through it.

In Paris, the bride and groom took a Cook's tour, window shopped, lunched at Webers and stayed at the Hotel Greffulhe. They didn't sleep; love clamored after every precious moment they had together. In the morning, their flight from Le Bourget airport was delayed for one-and-one-half hours due to fog. Up in the air, it was too noisy to talk but Mother enjoyed her box lunch while Father, sitting across the aisle, groaned with airsickness. She always was a good sailor. When they landed in London, a stewardess rushed up and said, "Are you all right? You've had a bumpy ride, haven't you?" They felt like pioneers in the air, although it was seventeen years since Louis Berliot first flew over the Channel.

That night, Elizabeth and Walter hosted a wedding banquet for twenty-six people in Kimbells' Hotel with a choice of consommé julienne, fillet of sole cardinal, lamb cutlets jardinière, roast chicken with chips and cress, maraschino cream ice, Charlotte vanilla, fruit salad, dessert and coffee. Father did not want to take Mother into Oxford House in winter so she planned to prepare her trousseau and say her farewells. She would join him in June.

The next day, Father stood transfixed on the deck of the Alaunia as his beautiful bride smiled at him roguishly from shore, waving a white silk scarf and blowing kisses. He couldn't feel sad even in parting. Surely the time would pass quickly with so much to do and anticipate. "I hope and pray we will bear up under the strain of lonesomeness," he wrote. "We have tasted the sweetness of married life and a wonderful experience lies ahead. We must philosophize and rationalize our fate and then things don't seem so bad." Each night they gave each other a big, imaginary hug.

Father had a risky trip ahead of him. He was planning to take a team of horses through the unbroken trail between the HBC line and Oxford House. This had never been done before but he told himself he was neither going to freeze nor starve to death. Upon arrival in Canada, he went home to Cookstown to tell his family he was married but Mary Jane showed no pleasure. Wilson told him not to worry about his trip; he always got through.

Passionate love letters from Mother now crossed the Atlantic Ocean. Father replied, "I feel as if hitherto I have been snatching such nourishment as I might from the crumbs you dropped but now you have placed before me a sumptuous feast. It is such a wonderful feeling to know there's one genuine girl who really loves you. Some people might think that what we have done is risky but we're not worried about that, are we? True marriage is a project for artists, not scientists."

In Winnipeg, Father inquired at the Parliament Buildings whether anyone in The Pas sold horses. While waiting for the answer, he stocked up on supplies and sent Mother a money order to buy herself a Paris frock, since she hadn't had time to find one on their honeymoon. He wanted to tell their news to his old flame, Esther, who was teaching school here, but didn't know how to do it. How could he have a date with her without disrupting the marital pattern? He solved the dilemma by telling Mother "his lordship" was asking "her ladyship's" permission and she was instantly granting it. Esther invited him to her landlady's for tea and he reciprocated by taking her out to the Chocolate Shoppe. She insisted he must bring his bride to stay with her in the spring but he declined, saying they had already agreed to go to a minister friend's home. Father reported to Mother that he had lunched with "a beautiful, charming, attractive, congenial and intelligent young lady but not nearly as beautiful, charming, attractive, congenial and intelligent as my wife."

The answer from The Pas was "No." Since it cost too much to freight a team of horses up the line, Father just bought one, Big Lad, who had a cheerful personality. At 3 a.m. they boarded a mixed freight train and for four days swayed and ricocheted up the west side of Lake Winnipeg. They traveled at night and had to shunt when the passenger train usurped the track. At a stopover in Swan River, Father knocked on the door of the parsonage and was just in time to address an area-wide girls' conference, talk to the Sunday School, assist at church and help entertain the Anglican minister and the local member of parliament over tea. Next day, the train passengers walked a quarter of a mile to a lumber camp for noon dinner.

In The Pas, Father lunched with the United Church minister who suggested he was an "abbreviated Irishman" who was really a Kells, Kelly or Kellogg. Father said "No." His line of Kells from Yorkshire, England, were blond so the name may have originally been Scandinavian. He was half Irish but on his mother's side. A Campbell had moved from the Scottish highlands to the southern fringes of northern Ireland in the 17th century, when the Crown was giving incentives to Protestants to go there to dilute the Catholic influence. Robert Campbell, a poor tenant farmer, emigrated to Canada to work on the Welland Canal, likely in 1827. A generous man, he brought out his siblings (including my great-grandfather, Matthew) and raised his sisters' children when they were orphaned.

Up beyond The Pas, Father and Big Lad, with their new toboggan and 800 pounds of supplies, were dumped out into a snowbank at Mile 137 (Wabowden.) It was midnight and -30 degrees, but an acquaintance-of-an-acquaintance from Beeton, Ontario, sheltered Father for the rest of the night. Early next morning, he made a deal with an Indian who was returning from jail to guide him to Cross Lake in return for pulling his possessions. Big Lad didn't want to have anything to do with that miserable-looking big worm (the toboggan.) The load kept upsetting on the crooked trail and they had to repack several times before they got going. It was hard, even with the wind in their backs, but they managed to jog into a camp at about 6 p.m. Just as the sun was setting, the moon rose in the sky and laughed at Father. "Never mind," it seemed to say, "I'm here."

They set out before sunrise and watched patches of forest light up here and there in a magical panorama of white, green and gold. As they followed the trail around a long, strung-out lake they expected at any moment to turn a corner and see the sun. Finally, Old Sol made his entrance in full glory. There was not a cloud in the sky. Not a sight except forest and snow. Not a sound but the slide of a toboggan and the crunch of a footstep and hoof. "Whatever else I am coming home to," Father thought, "I am returning to beautiful nature."

At Cross Lake, a letter from Mother was waiting for him. He sat out a three-day storm at the home of the missionaries before tackling the 130-mile trek on to Oxford House. With the authority of someone who had just come from England herself, his hostess said, "Your wife will love our winters." The route ahead was seldom trod by man and never before by horse. Big Lad would have to follow, rather than pull, so Father hired two natives with a team of dogs to break the trail.

For four days, they scrambled through the roughest of all bush, often on hand and knee, while Big Lad picked his way behind them like a perfect gentleman. Father had never had such cold hands or sore feet. It was terribly inconvenient trying to eat and sleep outside at -30 degrees. If you put up your hand to shield your face from the fire, the back of it burned while the palm froze. You could not sit or lie down because you had to keep rotating. The most irritating thing for Father was having to listen to the natives snore while he tossed and turned under his eiderdown, longing for a comfortable bed. He decided the difference must be due to generations of conditioning. They just curled up in little balls under their thin gray blankets, the way their dogs did under a layer of snow, and let their breath keep them warm.

Elizabeth Barrett Browning's lines, "Earth's crammed with heaven and every common bush afire with God," came to Father's mind. He could sort of layer the Indians' beliefs onto his own, as metaphors and similes. At night the northern lights danced like the spirits of the happy hunting grounds, darting about in shoots and waves, displaying the gentle color-tints of the rainbow. At a trapper's shack on the Carrot River, Father paid off the guides and sent them back to Cross Lake bearing a letter to Mother which he wrote by candlelight while sitting outdoors on a box. He loved incongruity.

The shack's owner, Absalom Ougemou, agreed to serve as guide for the rest of the journey. Father pushed Big Lad along because he knew he would sleep in his own stable that night. (Horses don't sleep when they are out on the trail.) Nelson, now twenty-five pounds heavier, and the Oxford House schoolchildren spied the horse and toboggan party coming into view and ran up the lake to greet them. The trip which now takes nine hours by car from Thompson, Manitoba, to Oxford House had taken seven days.

Father shared his happy news with his friends and gave out the little pieces of wedding cake he had carried in his pocket, as a reality check, all the way from The Cottage. Before he fell asleep, he wrote to Mother to tell her he was safely home and thanked God that he had a house, a roaring fire and a loving wife. The events of the past two months seemed like an improbable dream.

13

Mother Readies and Steadies Herself For an Oceanic Leap

Reactions to the wedding announcements poured in, assuring Mother of a warm welcome in Canada in the spring. Belated letters of reference told her Father had been a lifelong friend and assured her he was a wonderful person. Meanwhile, Father got this note from Ira Perkins: "You've sent my house into a riot! You went down to a count of nine like Tunney. A dash from the North Pole by dog team, tincanning across the Atlantic, putting a ring on the finger of the Queen of England, planting a kiss on her lips, taking her for an airplane trip, good-bye dearie, a dash back, fresh dog team and back at the North Pole before the fire went out. To think that I roomed for a year with a fellow like that!" Ezra, who had been following the tennis courtship since it began, sent just two words, "Who won?"

After all the excitement of getting married, Mother spent a miserable day at home alone with Elizabeth. Father had arrived on October 25th, wed her on November 2nd and left her on November 5th. She had married a man she had been with for only two weeks out of her whole life. She had agreed to be the lifelong work partner of a minister whom she had never heard preach. She was abandoning her family, her friends and her country. How could such a sensible person as herself have done such a thing?

"Mrs. Knell," as she was introduced at a singing

engagement, gave up drinking alcohol and smoking cigarettes in order to set a good example in her new role as a minister's wife. She had a lot of questions to ask of her husband, such as What color are your eyes? Should I bring my hockey stick? What about my silver chest? He told her she could bring anything she wanted, since the canoe was as commodious a method of travel as the train, but not golf clubs—and her hockey stick only if she was very attached to it. She should pack warm underwear in her "wanted" trunk, since the ocean crossing might be chilly. In reply to what rallying cry she could take up in place of Rule Britannia, he suggested Vive la Compagnie.

Father whet Mother's appetite for Canada by raving about two northern delicacies the Indians shared with him, moose nose and baked sturgeon. He had had the new toboggan converted into a cariole, the most comfortable conveyance imaginable. Blackie had given birth to a calf, Cinderella, and was providing cream for coffee and an ample supply of milk for the people. An earlier effort to bring in cows had failed when the Indian agent had said, "You will have to feed them sufficient hay." This was interpreted as, "some fish and hay." The Indians didn't have enough fish for themselves and their dogs, let alone cows.

As a faithful knight in the service of the church, Father was battling on amid frustrations and setbacks. Success depended on co-operation between church and government and on setting an example. Yet not one white man came to hear the Indians give their testimonies to Christ at the New Year's service. Indian agent Gordon had come to the reserve for the trial of a man for last fall's break-in and agreed to speak in church but he overslept. Father was deeply disappointed he had let the people down. His blood boiled when a Indian came back from Norway House empty-handed, due to a petty dispute at the HBC post.

The animal supply, especially beaver and muskrat, had dwindled. Traditional ways could not compete with the white trappers' methods of hunting an area out and then moving on. Some Indian hunters had to travel over an area of three hundred square miles to feed their families. George White, a white prospector and trapper who lived in a cabin at Knee Lake, was threatening and cursing them and not letting them get at their traps. The next time George came to stay at Mission House, Father told him he didn't want to be seen as harboring someone unfriendly to the Indians. George had to go up to sleep at the HBC instead.

For two years, Father had been imbuing Mother with the right attitudes to get along in Canada and now wrote, "You will have hosts of new friends, rich experiences in service and adventure and a home built on the foundation stones of love, sympathy and patience. Just because you are giving up so much, I am going to try doubly hard to make things pleasant and nice for you. You have all the qualities that spell success and need not feel a single tremor."

Mother was making an impression on both sides of the ocean. At Oxford House, Mr. Gordon looked at her picture and said, "She has strong eyes." The Indian mothers asked who she was and Father answered with the Cree words, kitche okimow squao (queen.) They said "eh" knowingly and asked exactly how big she was. She was also the toast of Portsmouth, juggling appointments and engagements. Most difficult of all to part with were the Portsea girls, who had become her friends. Three of them came to the café for extra help with their lines for the Christmas concert. Two of them expected to become domestic servants but the third, a hawker's daughter, wrote stories and wanted to go on stage. At the annual bazaar at Wesley Chapel, the four Misses Greene, spinsters who ran a private school Mother attended when very small, said they had always known she would be a missionary and made her promise to write a book.

George White had stopped bothering the Indians and the unaccustomed quiet made them even more uneasy. They alerted Father who, with a sense of foreboding, trekked with the HBC factor and a guide out to George's cabin, fearing the worst. They found his frozen body lying on the floor with his rifle beside it. They sent for the RCMP who came up to investigate and determined that he had killed himself. Father helped bring the corpse in, thawed it out on his diningroom table and fixed it up for a funeral. This tragedy was a big blow to the small community of white men around the reserve who stayed in each other's homes, argued vociferously, cut each other's hair and shared three bathing suits. Last year, George had given a talk in church on how to make sourdough bread. This year, his hopes were dashed when the gold claims he staked were proven worthless.

In April, the Indian families came in from winter camp dragging their dead family members behind them. Father figured he could cut thirty days off his and Mother's separation by going out over the ice, rather than waiting for the thaw as planned. The Portsmouth people would think Canada an inhospitable place if spring didn't come until June. He asked Mother if she could set sail in early May and sent her the money to reserve cabin-class passage.

On April 16th, Father set out with a guide on the trail he had been hacking to the railway line, hoping to visit Cree encampments along the way. Instead, they got lost for a whole day, until they found a fishing camp at 2 a.m. After resting up, Father felt so good he walked ahead of the dogs all the way to Pikwitonei. The minister's wife pressed his trousers and he helped her husband with the Sunday service.

In Winnipeg, a marconigram from Mother informed Father she would arrive on the Ausonia on May 14th. He had expected her to be on the Metagami on May 4th, so now he had time to stay a few days in Toronto and also go home to visit his mother. But in Toronto, on May 2nd, he got word from Clara that an unsigned telegram had arrived in Cookstown saying, "Come quickly. Metagami docks May 4th." Father was mystified but decided he'd better hurry on to Montreal. When he got to Ernie Taylor's home there, he told him he had sent the telegram. Meanwhile, Mary Jane's temper flared. Not only was her daughter-in-law English (as if a Canadian girl wasn't perfectly good enough), but also she sent imperious telegrams so that her son didn't even visit her. Father cooled his heels for ten days in Montreal, painting a baby carriage and speaking to YMCA youth groups.

Clutching a bouquet of lilies of the valley, Mother waved good-bye to her family and England. Just before her boat pulled out, a friend from the café had a wedding present delivered to the boat—a thirty-piece tea set of fine china decorated with silhouettes of fairies. The steward said it could not land in Canada. The straw it was packed in might carry foot and mouth disease so Mother repacked it in the warm underwear in her trunk. She got to know the ship's recreation director who told her the Ausonia was carrying Polish and Czech emigrants in steerage. Mother was curious to see what they looked like and recorded in her journal, "They are extraordinary folk who lie about the deck in weird positions, some of them on top of each other. The smell of garlic around their cabins is appalling." They packed it in with their clothes to ward off disease. The former captain of the Lusitania was at the helm and invited Mother to sit at his table.

The sea was calm, with steady rain and misty patches, as the ship entered the St. Lawrence River and Mother saw the contours of a rugged, barren-looking land studded with tall pine and fir trees huddling together. Gray rocks interrupted brown grass and vegetation. Little villages nestled near the shore, each distinguished by its tiny church and spire. White houses with bright, green roofs stood out against a dark background. At Father Point, a pinnace arrived bearing a Canadian pilot and the mail, including letters for Mother from Father and Walter.

Father saw the Ausonia come into view and had no trouble spotting likely the last war bride from the First World War. She was wearing a fur coat and beehive hat purchased especially for Canada. On one arm she was bearing the dozen red roses he had cabled to her in Quebec City and, in the other, she was cradling a newspaper package. That was his girl—so refined and yet so realistic! The package contained the dress she wore at the ship's farewell party and had left hanging in her cabin cupboard, where the steward noticed it. At Customs, she had to separate what she needed from what could be sent on so she retrieved her underwear from her china in public on the station platform. She called this her "first housekeeping problem in Canada."

Father immediately delivered on his promise to provide her with a host of new experiences: lunch with the Taylors in Montreal and a bear hug from Ezra in Kingston. Then, dinners at Clara's and close friends' homes in Toronto, plus seeing the sights: the university, the normal school (where Clara was studying to become a teacher), Eaton's and the board of missions. At the home of superintendent Barner, where they slept, Mother had her first taste of creamed corn.

The next day, Clifton drove them thirty miles north through sparsely settled land. Mother was fascinated to see farms separated by fences, not hedges, and wood-frame houses with big chimneys—a sign of the central heating she had heard about. After driving up a beautiful maple lane to a big, comfortable house, they got a raucous welcome from the dog and the parrot, which Father had brought back from Mexico. Mother met Mary Jane, Mabel, Wilson, his wife Maggie and their children, Mary and Albert. She hardly recognized her cousin Bernard in overalls, digging a hole for a new pump underneath the windmill. Father put on his old hat and cautioned her to stay out of the mud while he showed her around, leaving the women to prepare a hearty meal. After dinner, they gave Mother her wedding presents: a broad-bladed serving knife and other pieces of sterling silver, beautiful table linens made of lace and damask, Pyrex cooking ware and a tortoise-shell dresser set. Mabel gave her an eiderdown made out of wool from her pet lamb, and the money for six hens.

Although Father had said Mary Jane would be a kind and intelligent friend, Mother was not to find her so. She had not written to welcome her into the family, as had Clara and Mabel, and seemed to be nursing a grudge. In an effort to get into her good graces, Mother said she was "green" and didn't even know how to iron a man's shirt. Mary Jane heated up an iron on the wood stove, fitted it with a handle, put up the ironing board, got a shirt, and sat down with the other women to be entertained.

It was a great release for them to laugh at Mother's struggle but she was mortified.

Mary Jane could not understand why the Wards had sent Bernard to them. He had no interest in nor aptitude for farm work. These Wards pressured people! His real name was Jack and that's what she called him. He seemed to imagine the family's two 100-acre farms (one belonging to her and one to Wilson) to be far grander than they were. Of course none of Mary Jane's underlying grumbling erupted, and Father didn't go looking for trouble. If he had any suspicions, he just sloughed them off. Mother drew Father into another room for a whispered conversation behind the closed door but he assured her they liked her. Then she sat alone in a corner of the front room and read a book.

Father drove Mother over to visit other relatives' homes on luxuriant hundreds of acres of rolling, verdant land. She was most impressed with the beautiful cellars where potatoes, vegetables and fuel were stored. The meals were informal, compared to those in England, but were served on fine-quality china and table linens and always included cake. "The Canadian woman runs a home, raises children and yet finds time to study and even take university courses," Mother wrote home. "There is no place like this for making you realize you are essentially a man or a woman with a mind and body to be used in good, healthy exercise. Canada is a wonderful place if you are prepared to work." She sat on a horse, watched a windmill go up, posed for a picture with the sheared lamb and was welcomed from the pulpit of Cookstown United Church on Sunday.

Fortunately, Mother could not see what lay ahead. Some weeks after this visit, Bernard had a nervous breakdown. He became very religious and gave the family a terrible fright lest he do himself harm. They got him to hospital, with the help of the police constable and a neighbor, and contacted his parents. He was put on a boat bound for England as soon as he was well enough to travel. He got better but, a few years later, stepped in front of a car and was killed. The Wards thought these nervous breakdowns must come from the Wooller side of the family.

Walter and his brother, Jack, had married two sisters. My great-grandfather, William James Wooller, electrical foreman at the Portsmouth Dockyards in Thomas Edison's day, had thrown the family tree on the fire. (Colonel Fairfax, Oliver Cromwell's right-hand man, was one of the ones whose name got singed.) To William, this was all "a lot of snob nonsense." He himself was the huge, blond son of a Yorkshire merchant seaman who drowned.

14

A Trip By Canoe Along the Old Fur Trade Route To Oxford House

After leaving the farm, Mother and Father hopped off the Toronto-bound bus at Richmond Hill so he could show her his boarding-house on his old preaching charge. It was a surprise party! Everyone burst out singing Blest Be the Tie That Binds as they arrived and well-wishers kept dropping in until 10:30 p.m. The next day at Wymilwood, the wood-paneled girls' residence at Victoria College, my parents hosted a reception for forty of Father's friends before boarding The National for Winnipeg.

The scenery changed from green farmland to pines, firs, rock, brown grass, streams, lakes and swamps. Huts, a lumber camp, floating logs and isolated railway stations flashed by. At Hornepayne they stayed with the Levi Atkinsons, who used to be missionaries at Oxford House. To Mother, this railway town of 1200 looked like a scene from the movies. Men were sitting on the steps outside wooden shops. Little children competing in a sports day to celebrate Queen Victoria's birthday (the 24th of May) were wearing long trousers à la Jackie Coogan or wide-brimmed straw hats à la Broncho Bill. Mother was three hundred miles away from the nearest highway and surrounded by bush yet didn't feel at all isolated as she chatted with Mrs. Atkinson about what winter clothes to buy.

In Winnipeg, Mother plunged into vive-la-compagnie life, United-Church style. The annual conference of the Lake

Winnipeg Presbytery of the Manitoba Conference of the United Church of Canada was meeting in Knox Church. While Father attended business sessions morning, afternoon and night, Mother joined the ministers' wives group and sampled the Canadian specialties of cantaloupe sundae and pumpkin pie. Esther showed her around the city and the two women found, over tea, that they had much in common. A shopping spree with Father for a cedar chest (his wedding present to her), a year's supply of food and household goods, an organ, a canoe and six hens capped "an exceedingly kind week," in Mother's words.

From the conference, they rushed by taxi to Selkirk to catch the season's first run of the steamer Wolverine (The Wolf.) They sat like royalty on the upper deck with two prospectors, looking back at their zigzag path in the sunset as they progressed up the Red River to Lake Winnipeg. The two hundred and fifty miles to Warren Landing took one and one-half days. At the fishing village on Snake Island, Mother met the native postmistress, who had eleven children, and a ninety-year-old man who was the postcard image of a North American Indian yet claimed to be the first white man on the lake. The hens came through by laying two eggs which the ship's cook was glad to get. At a difficult, rocky channel near the Berens River Reserve, wooden crosses marked the spot where a missionary couple, their four children and two Indian guides had drowned.

Passengers going beyond Warren Landing transferred to a smaller steamboat. It negotiated for three-and-one-half hours with rocks and islands in the pale-green waters of Playgreen River and Playgreen Lake. Anna Gaudin was standing on the shore in Norway House to greet my parents and take them to Mission House. Father's Indian friends, Isaac Mason and Geordie Grieves, were waiting for them too. For four decades, Anna had dedicated herself to giving the Indians at Nelson House and Cross Lake nursing care and first aid. She told Mother how rough it had been and how she had lost three infant daughters and an infant son to disease. While my parents stayed with the Gaudins for five days, waiting for their freight to arrive and the winds to change, they felt very at home. The Indian agent, the RCMP officer, the principal and the entire teaching staff of the school all invited them for meals. At the hospital, the doctor went over their medical supplies with them and taught Father how to give injections and pull teeth.

By six a.m. on June 11, 1928, two 16-foot canvas canoes, equipped with oars and sails as well as paddles, were packed and ready. The school launch offered them a tow over to Hope Island and Mother and Father got in. They had not gone many yards when one canoe started going in all directions because of the unbalanced load. All of Mother's belongings were on the verge of dumping. Isaac and Geordie jumped into the water and, after a struggle, managed to climb into the canoe and sail it. After having tea at Monkmans' on the island, they departed with a "care package" of oranges, cream and eggs.

Two Indian transporters shoved off in the freight canoe first, sailing eastward along the Nelson River to Sea Falls, Hairy Lake, the Echimamish River, the Height of Land and Robinson Portage, where they would wait up. This route had been plied by Hudson Bay Company York boats up until 1923 and the wooden railway used to roll the boats over the portage was still there. An oral historian of the Cree, named H.G. Wells, had told Father that, many centuries ago, a group of Crees had separated from the main Algonquin tribe on the east coast of the continent. Driven west by famine, they came to the prairies where they encountered hostile Sioux. The Cree fled in birchbark canoes to get away from their enemies, who did not have this technology, and opened up the whole territory from Ontario to the Rocky Mountains.

The second canoe was arranged with Geordie in the bow, the crate of hens behind him, my parents facing the hens and Isaac in the stern. Luggage was stuffed in between them. They sailed, shot small rapids, then stopped at Sea Falls Portage and crossed stepping-stones to find a place to eat (and, in Mother's case, change out of her skirt.) Farther on at Hairy Lake, named for the reeds sticking out of it, they saw flocks of ducks, geese and swans, and three canoes from God's Lake. The sail jibed and came off the mast in the strong wind but the men got it back on. They stopped at the mouth of the Echimamish for tea, then went on and pitched their tent on spongy soil at 8 p.m. They had come forty-five miles.

Mother woke early to the sound of pounding rain but it stopped by 8 a.m. and they rowed out into a pretty world. The dark waters of the narrow river were overhung by thick willows which brushed against her and gave her a shut-in feeling, as if there was no life around. Then they came to an opening at some small, impassable rapids. When the men tried to pull the canoe through by getting out and standing on rocks, Isaac fell in and got wet. They stopped for lunch early and built a fire so he could dry out. The northern scenery of rapids, rocks and towering trees was captivating Mother. As they got going again, a chorus of frogs accompanied them past marshlands with low bushes and fir trees beyond. The sun shone, the wind blew and the river broadened. At a shallow stretch, where the river was scarcely more than a creek, the oars struck mud and the canoe grounded. Father helped get it going by walking and paddling.

A forest fire had ravished the land around and a submerged rock ripped a hole in the bottom of the canoe, causing it to leak slightly at the seam. At a spot where they had to get out and walk, Mother slipped and sat in the water so had to change in the bush. They battled upstream against a head-wind and adverse current until they rested and drank tea at 2:30 p.m. In the next hour they reached the Height of Land, where they portaged to another creek which flowed downstream into a wider river. Mother faced into a cold, north wind as the hens pecked at her straw hat from behind. After logging forty more miles that day, they struck camp, had supper, said their prayers and went to sleep.

The men began to stir at 3:30 a.m. so my parents got up; it hardly got dark at all at this time of year. They set off at 5:30 a.m. and were hailed by a Swedish trapper in another canoe who called out to Father, "You're going to get it! You're late!" They reached Robinson Portage at 6:15 a.m. to find the two transporters who had gone ahead asleep on the beach. They had pushed their canoe and the freight over the portage in the wooden railway's two steel-wheeled carriages. Mother could hear the rushing sound of Robinson Falls, a long stretch of rapids, but didn't go over to see them because of the wet grass and mosquitoes. Father helped her walk over the slippery, two-mile portage while the Indians pulled the second canoe-load up the steep incline, then restrained it on the way down. By 7: 45 a.m. the two canoes were reloaded and being swept along the twelve-mile extent of Robinson Lake by a fair wind. They stopped for meals whenever Isaac got hungry and today lunch was at 10 a.m.

After they started sailing again, they encountered the Oxford House Chief and his son who were taking a sick man by canoe to the Norway House Hospital. Around noon they reached High Hill Portage, a steep hill over a mile high. They carried their belongings over, reloaded and shoved off again in only one and one-quarter hours. Now they headed northeast into Moriah Lake, famous for its echoing cliffs. They stopped for tea before entering Pine Lake because a strong wind and dark clouds overhead looked very threatening. They could see rough waves ahead as they lingered in the small river. The skies burst suddenly so they took cover under their macintoshes during a ten-minute inundation. Now Windy Lake calmed down and they sailed steadily ahead until they encountered a head-wind. Then they camped for the night in the shelter of a sharp point.

Next morning, on the other side of Windy Lake, they arrived at the gorgeous rapids in the little river feeding into Oxford Lake, where blue waters plummeted over mossy green stones. They shot some of the rapids and portaged others as huge jackfish swam in front of the tall, green trees. They were reloading at the last portage, Waypinahpanns, when two canoes landed. It was a Cree custom to paddle out to greet new arrivals. The Oxford House men shook hands solemnly with Mother and then, just as solemnly, with Isaac and Geordie, whom they had known all their lives. How she was amused and savored her new freedom! In English society, so many little things, such as shaking hands with a person you had already met, simply "were not done." At 9:30 a.m. they entered forty-mile-long Oxford Lake and sailed at such a thrilling pace that Mother's hat box flew overboard. Geordie had to retrieve the tennis balls, oranges and other odds and ends it held. At 3 p.m. they caught the first glimpse on the horizon of the rock outcroppings at Oxford House, altitude 700 ft. At 4:45 p.m. they stopped on a rocky island to tidy up and at 6 p.m. they arrived.

The Indian Chief, many of the reserve's four hundred members and Nelson Gaudin were standing on shore to greet them. Mother felt shy but, in no time, Father had her on her feet, out of the canoe and shaking hands. They walked up the path and he carried her over the threshold of Mission House. Before they could finish eating supper, the two Hudson Bay Company clerks dropped in and, then, the Hudson Bay factors. Mrs. Davidson had come out from Scotland as a bride a year ago and had found her winter as the only white woman on the reserve difficult. She had just returned from a visit to the doctor and a prolonged rest in Winnipeg. Dulas and Alice McIvor and their six-year-old daughter, Effie, also dropped in. After they left, Mother and Father lingered in the doorway looking at the spectacular color display in the sky made by a distant forest fire.

Mother saw the other Oxford House women going out to their fishing nets every day and setting rabbit snares in the bush. When the hunters came in with moose hides the women scraped them in a frame and tanned them by the fire. They made them into beautifully embroidered moccasins, slippers, mitts and parkas which were snapped up by tourists in Norway House. The women dried strips of moose and deer meat to make pemmican (dried meat pounded and made into cakes with fat and dried berries) and they threaded fish on sticks to smoke it for winter dog food.

The native women dressed in the 18th-century style of shawls and long skirts which the Scottish Hudson Bay factors' wives had worn. They were the first persons to come here bearing bibles and practising the habits of praying and hymn-singing. On her first Sunday in the Oxford House church, the beauty of the Cree language impressed Mother as Isaac read the scriptures. Father read the same passage in English and the hymns were sung in both languages at once. Mother thought of the text which had inspired her to devote her life to mission work: *Other sheep have I and they too must be brought into the fold.*

The British Wesleyan Methodist Church had originally been invited to these territories by the HBC. Its labor force was being sucked south of the border by the magical appeal of circuit preachers and their book, the Bible. The Rev. James Evans, who dressed in a buckskin jacket and had long hair, opened the Methodist mission at Norway House in 1840. He had been preaching to the Ojibways in southern Ontario for two years and spoke their language. His travels to the isolated settlements in northern Manitoba now spawned a religious movement of native, charismatic preachers. He invented a syllabic alphabet of nine characters which, when turned four ways, stood for the thirty-six sounds in the Cree language. He taught it to them by carving the characters into a birch tree, so they called him The Man Who Can Make the Birchbark Talk. Today this language still unites the Cree people, who have a very high rate of literacy. In 1841 Evans printed a Cree hymnbook, the first book printed in western Canada, by using clay, sturgeon oil, soot scraped from his chimney, lead foil from the lining of tea chests and a leather-press. A Cree copy of St. John's Gospel and other passages of the Bible soon followed.

The story goes that Evans opposed the HBC for making Indian employees work on Sundays. He also condemned the behavior of the head factor in Norway House for choosing a woman for himself from among the wives of each chief in the area. The HBC strongly opposed Evans's interference. He was accused of having sexually molested a sick woman, an allegation difficult to refute in a court where the head factor was also the judge. Just then, Evans accidentally killed one of his close Indian associates while placing a loaded rifle into a canoe. He was sent home to England and died of a heart attack almost immediately, at age forty-five. Oxford House played a role in this tragedy when, years later, a woman on her deathbed called for the Norway House missionary. She confessed that she had been bribed to make the accusation of sexual molestation against Evans. His Ojibway assistant, H. B. Steinhauer, who was also an ordained minister, established a resident mission at Oxford House in 1851 and the reserve converted to Christianity in 1900. The ashes of Evans, a hero to the Cree people, were buried in a ceremony at Norway House in 1955.

Settling into married life, Mother sewed curtains on her treadle machine while Father planted seeds. They and Nelson shared the two-bedroom log bungalow, finished with beautiful hardwood floors and white siding, which the Church provided. Most of the Indians lived cramped up in teepees or shacks. The mission team organized a field day for the last day of school with events such as climbing the pole, threading the needle and scrambling for sweets.

One of the first callers was Napao Munroe, who wanted advice on what to name his baby. Names were very important; they indicated a connection with another person which might be helpful in times of need. After listening to suggestions, he decided to call his son Walter, the first name of Mother's father, and Gordon, the surname of the Indian agent. The christening ceremony gave Mother an occasion to use some of her silver and lace wedding presents. At least a dozen Indians came every day to barter food, get first aid or other help, ask advice, arrange a baptism or wedding or have a tooth pulled. Mother discovered that the native remedy of wet tea leaves worked on burns.

Two of her favorite callers were the Curleyheads. Alice always managed to charm a little extra out of Father in the way of supplies. David had lost the use of both legs, due to arthritis, so had to sit down and push himself along with both arms. When he was young, he had been stranded alone for six weeks on an island. He had his Cree hymnbook with him so memorized all the hymns and never lost hope he would be saved. He kept himself alive by eating seagulls' eggs. Another favorite was Bobbie Chubb, who liked to brag. He told Mother he disciplined his children by locking the door of his house at

10 p.m. every night. Then he looked at his watch and said, "To-night I have locked myself out."

Seventy families (one hundred and forty-seven church members) were in Father's pastoral care. In the past year he had had eight baptisms, three weddings and ten funerals. His annual salary was $1297 from the Church, plus $50 from the government for serving as medical dispenser. Mother balanced the books of the mission, one of the Church's most successful. By accounting for every last tablespoonful of flour she reported a surplus of 72 cents.

On the way back from a baby's funeral with a coffin in the canoe, Mother and Father tossed their wolf/Husky dog, Byng, into the water because of his disrespectful panting.

Mother was trying to figure out how to fillet a trout as smoke from the distant forest fire wafted in through the kitchen window. Just then Father spotted two canoe-loads of visitors far up the lake so he ran and got Eva Bell, his Indian housekeeper, to help Mother. Fish and potatoes were prepared, scones baked, beds made up and oranges and milk set out on the diningroom table by the time the canoes arrived. They contained the missionary couple from God's Lake and their two daughters, a couple with a baby, and two prospectors. One of the latter had a pair of lynx pups he was planning to sell to the Winnipeg Zoo. The prospectors' canoe had an engine on it and was towing the other one. Two mining instructors from the University of Toronto were already sleeping on the verandah but they moved out into a tent with Nelson as Mother shuffled things around until everyone had a place. She and Father slept on the floor. Fourteen people sat down for breakfast at 7 a.m. before the guests took to their canoes again.

The forest fire got worse and advanced closer. Mother stayed home from church, because of a bilious attack, but was roused from her bed by the sound of the fire. It was terribly frightening to see. Great volumes of smoke were rising into the air. Across the river, flames were leaping high and licking the tops of the evergreens. They caught fire, burned brightly for a few moments and fell off.

Practically all of northern Manitoba was on fire. A native forestry ranger commandeered one hundred prospectors and trappers to fight the fire in the Island Lake district, then flew up to Oxford House and directed a group of men all night. The danger was not so much from the fire across the river as from one behind them at Back Lake. The pilot said he would fly up there to check it out and drop a note on his way back if they were in danger. Meanwhile, the men rescued the people who lived on the other side of the river and prevented the fire from leaping across. The wind changed and the pilot dropped nothing when he flew over, to everyone's huge relief.

Near the beginning of August, the hunters, trappers, transporters, guides and other workers belonging to the Oxford House band returned home. Since the white man frowned on dancing and pagan beliefs, treaty time replaced the traditional ceremonies held to seek the totem god's protection and blessing. When the plane carrying Dr. Turpel and Indian agent Gordon arrived, things got underway. The doctor examined the people, pulled teeth, prescribed medicine and vaccinated everyone against smallpox. Father accompanied him and received instructions on how to follow up with certain cases. Mother visited the women who were sick and a teen-age girl who had had a stillborn baby, the "farewell present" of the HBC clerk who had been transferred and gone out with Father the previous fall.

With Mr. Gordon presiding, the men elected their chief and two councilors. All male members of the tribe sat in council to decide questions, big and small, and serve as a court. Father had been trying to persuade the Indians not to re-elect the same chief year after year but to no avail. It was a very heavy job. This year the elections had to be held twice because the Chief was sick and resigned after one day. Mr. Gordon handed out the government annuity of $5 to each person and spoke in church on treaty Sunday.

After the treaty party flew off, a heap of big bags and boxes appeared on the grassy green and the Cree gathered around them in family groups with their baskets and containers. The

Chief, the Councilors and other prominent men each took a sack of sugar, flour, etc. and went around the circle measuring the food out a cupful at a time. When the long, drawn-out ceremony was over, they feasted and danced until late into the night. Treaty week was jammed full with weddings and baptisms. Father thought this time of jollification was good for the Indians, with everyone able to buy trinkets that caught the eye and stirred the imagination. Mother watched the men buy new sweaters which they pulled over their old ones for added warmth. She counted how many they were wearing by looking at the colors showing through the holes.

As the treaty party was preparing to leave the reserve, Mother drew Dr. Turpel aside and told him she had not had any regular menstrual periods since she came to Canada. Now she was getting a "bloody show" (medical terminology) from time to time. He said she might be pregnant or her symptoms might be due to the radical changes she had made in country and lifestyle. If her symptoms got worse, she should come down to the hospital to see him.

15

A Pregnant Mother's Winter Cariole Ride Delivers Ecstasy

The bleeding continued so Father, Isaac and Jimmy delivered Mother by canoe to the Norway House Hospital in early September. Dr. Turpel examined her and said she was expecting a baby but there was a danger of a miscarriage. Luckily, the prone position in the canoe for five days had been the best thing for her. The doctor prescribed another ten days' bed rest in the hospital and that cleared the trouble up completely. An airplane was flying up to Oxford House so Mother was able to send a message to Father, saying she was well enough to return. If it wasn't too late for him to come down, they wouldn't have to spend the winter apart. Father and his two guides promptly jumped into a canoe.

On the way home, Isaac misjudged the force of the wind out on Oxford Lake and yelled "We're not going to make it!" while Jimmy thumped his chest and said "My heart's going like this!" Somehow they overpowered the waves, got the canoe under control and made it to shore, almost completely swamped with water. Soaking wet, they got going again. As they pulled into Oxford House on September 27th the first big snowstorm of the season, and of Mother's life, was in close pursuit.

A father of two small children fell through the ice and drowned in October and an outbreak of chicken pox afflicted the reserve. My parents had no party to celebrate their first anniversary. After the epidemic abated, the McIvors and

Davidsons came over to visit and listen to radio concerts. Wilson arrived from Cookstown and helped Father with the church services, wood-hauling and last of the haying. It was his first trip away from Ontario and, on the trail in, a red beard emerged to mock his blond hair. He brought letters containing news of Eric's wedding to Doris Parker, and of King George V's illness. Mother formed the Oxford House Girls' Club and started to teach them how to sing together as a choir for the Christmas concert. Father bought her a wolf skin for $25 to keep her warm.

Mother thought it would be best for their baby if it were born in a hospital, with a doctor attending, and Father agreed this was a sensible idea. Among the texts he chose for his sermons were *Be ye not over-anxious* and *The woman with the issue of blood.* He had to get Mother out safely before her due date in the depth of the deep winter freeze but, in the meantime, the busy Christmas season was looming. She was in good health but he was haunted by an experience he had had when he was a student minister at Warren Landing. The doctor had asked him to help take a pregnant, young Cree woman who was suffering from toxemia to hospital. She was screaming from pain and was so delirious she had to be restrained. They did not get there in time to save her.

Father hitched Big Lad up to the cariole to pull Mother over to the Davidsons' for tea but she came down with a terrible cold. She was unable to help with the Christmas concert and Mrs. Davidson had to replace her as organist on Christmas Sunday. All the hunters came in from their winter camps to trade their furs and attend the Christmas church service. Afterwards, Father was happily surprised to find Mother up on her feet and simmering one of the hens (two of them had been eaten by dogs) on the stove. Later that day, Father married the widow of the former chief, who had just died, to the new chief. The HBC clerks, Stanley and Henry, came on New Year's to eat a rooster Stanley's father had sent up from Norway House.

Father persuaded Regan Munroe, the young Indian he had married on short notice the summer before, not to go back to the hunt but to be their guide for the trip. Jack Gordon, the Indian agent's son who succeeded Nelson as school-teacher, agreed to look after the work of the mission while they were away. The deal was that Father would lend him Tommy and the cariole to take to Norway House to spend the holidays with his parents. After he got back, Tommy would need a few days' rest before Mother and Father set out.

Tommy sensed his master was feeding and patting him especially attentively, examining his harness and the cariole with extra care. He knew he was going to be entrusted to do something only an exceptional horse like himself could do and he would give it his all. Mother was getting excited about the prospect of "dashing through the snow in a one-horse open sleigh," even though Tommy didn't have bells or a bob-tail.

It was -30 degrees on the morning of Jan. 15, 1929, when Mother emerged from Mission House, after spending more time choosing her wardrobe and dressing than she had for any Mayor's Ball or Royal Event. She was wearing her fur coat, now with a big hood attached, a pair of Father's breeches and a pair of winter moccasins. Pieces of eiderdown, her own invention, were folded around her ankles in the shape of feet. Underneath, her delicate condition's first layer of fortification against the cold was a set of long, combination underwear. On top of this, she wore a sweater, a pair of Father's long, woolen pants and two pairs of heavy socks. Her hands and forearms were covered with the Indian gauntlets Mr. Gordon had given her as a hostess present at treaty time. In short, she was very sensibly dressed for what lay ahead.

Father put his finishing touch on the loaded cariole and helped Mother into her first-class accommodations. The big toboggan was 8' 2" long and 2' 3" wide; it had a wooden back rest about two-thirds of the way along its length and a wooden frame to hold up its canvas sides. Behind the back rest, Father placed a bag of oats for Tommy, a grub box containing enough food for three people for six days and a jerry (chamber-pot) discreetly concealed in a sack. On the cariole itself, he had carefully arranged Regan's bag of clothes and blanket, his own and Mother's two small kit bags, a box and a suitcase. All this was covered with an ample mattress of hay. Father tucked Mother in with a huge, khaki, canvas-covered eiderdown underneath her and another one on top.

The trip had been delayed for several days, due to blowing snow, but now the weather had cleared and the sun was shining. The route to the hospital, one hundred and eighty miles to the southeast (twenty miles shorter than in summer) lay mainly over rivers and lakes frozen several feet deep with a layer of snow on top. Mother sat semi-reclined on top of the load, while Father jogged alongside holding Tommy's reins and Regan ran ahead to blaze the trail. Basic to Mother's comfort was the fact that, from her vantage point, Father was always in sight. She was madly in love with him, had complete faith in him and would follow him anywhere. He was "awfully good to her and wonderfully strong and fit in both wind and limb" (quotes from her journal.) She had with her a rubber hot-water bottle and some chocolates, just in case she should have to give birth prematurely along the way. As they got going, one of her eyelashes froze to the fur trim on her hood and she watched Father's face frame with rime formed by his moist, warm breath landing on his collar and cap.

Twenty minutes out, they stopped to say goodbye to Dulas and Alice McIvor at their store on The Point. This educated Cree woman had become Mother's best friend and was very concerned about her. Mother did not stir from her embalmment in the cariole so she came out to wish her well before they went on. At mid-day, the toboggan party found shelter by the side of Oxford Lake, gathered wood, built a huge fire and unpacked the grub box of its contents: two frying pans, two tea pails and frozen food. The whole glob of cooked meat, beans, bread and butter was dumped into the frying pan to thaw out and heat through. Mother had never eaten out in the cold before and was hungry. No sooner had she put the steel fork into her mouth than it froze and tore away the skin, making her lip bleed.

They traveled on but by sundown were still out on Oxford Lake so camped on shore around 5 p.m. After their meal and prayers, Mother tried to go to sleep in the cariole but woke up every hour feeling cramped. The fire roasted her on one side while she froze on the other, so she had to keep constantly revolving. Father and Regan made themselves beds of spruce boughs on the ground and rolled up in their bedding. Regan slept soundly in his single blanket but Father not a wink in his eiderdown. Well-blanketed, Tommy stood watch, tied to a tree under the starry sky amid the softly sighing spruces. A nose-bag prevented him from wasting even one of his precious oats and he had eaten his nightly ration of hay from Mother's mattress. Over the past three winters, he had taken Father over seven hundred and fifty square miles of territory to visit isolated camps, spending over twenty nights wide-awake like this in the open.

Father got the fire going at 3 a.m. and at 5 a.m. they ate breakfast. Mother promptly threw up and blamed all the rotating between heat and cold for the loss. They pushed on and crossed three small portages around rapids, which let Mother ease her backbone and stretch her legs. These narrow bush paths were more sheltered than the open trail. After camping at mid-day, she felt ill and miserable all afternoon, being sore, cold and shaken by the motion. Her mattress was getting thinner as they progressed! They went over more portages of one-half mile or so in length from lake to lake.

By the time they stumbled into the log house "of no great dimensions" owned by Bobbie Chubb on Pine Lake, it seemed like heaven to Mother. It had an outer livingroom with an open fireplace ventilated by a hole in the roof. That night all seven of the Indians—Bobbie, his wife, two sons, two daughters and Regan—slept on the floor, while my parents were given the inner room, which had a stove and a built-in bed. Mother felt pretty sick and they contemplated staying for one or two days. However, after a good night's sleep she was feeling fairly fit, so they parted from their cheery hosts. They pushed on all day and stopped just for meals. By now Mother had got her trail legs but was stiff from lying so long in the same position and had a sore end to her spine. Towards evening, they walked the four-mile length of Robinson Portage and, after sunset, struck an empty old shack. It was low and drafty but "four walls and a roof are something to be grateful for even if you do hit your head every time you stand up," she wrote later. They lit the dilapidated stove but had forgotten to bring candles. It was cold sleeping on the floor but Mother's fur coat kept her warm. Father didn't have a fur coat, let alone eiderdown foot wrappings, and suffered.

After an early start the next day, they reached a Cree winter camp at noon. Having dinner, resting and warming herself in a very clean house put Mother on a high. She felt so good she gave one of her chocolates to each of the five children scampering about. That night, Regan led the cariole party to the cabin of John Kirkness, a hermit who lived miles away from anyone on Molson Lake. Part native and part white, he was well educated, had served in the war and had worked at lumber camps. His wall was decorated with a home-made calendar and recipes for pie. He, too, had no candles so he put melted butter in a saucer with a piece of cloth to give light. That night, Mother and the three men all slept on the floor of the one room. Father's help at a little undressing underneath their eiderdown made it ripple mysteriously.

They rose before sunrise to face a big dip in the temperature and yet sixty miles to go. Not far out on the lake, Father's nose and chin froze and Mother was horrified, expecting them to drop off. He explained that this was not unusual in the north, the spots would go white and then develop into a blister and sore, like a bad sunburn. When they got to Charlie Saunders' house, the last on the trail, they thawed themselves out and ate. Not wanting to spend another night in the open, they pushed on. They camped briefly around 6:30 p.m. at a point with tall trees and plenty of dry wood where they could build a fire and eat grub. Regan carried a fire-bag of coals from stop to stop so he could get the fire going quickly. On a night such as this in January, 1841, Evans had written in his diary, "Water from a kettle nearly boiling, poured into a tin plate to a depth of about one-half inch, becomes frozen in one-and-one-half minutes at—42 degrees." The cariole party didn't have a thermometer and didn't have time to do experiments. They just drank three or four cups of tea which magically stayed warm and invigorated them. At 10 p.m. they stopped again to rest Tommy, and Mother managed to sleep for over an hour.

At midnight, they rested at the portage between the Muscataban and Nelson rivers and lit a fire, supervised by the crescent moon. Out again on the trail at 2:30 a.m., it suddenly became dark and they got lost. This had happened a few times before but Regan always found the way by stopping the procession and walking a few paces, first in one direction, then in each of the others. He studied the snow, the vegetation, the trees, the wind and the skies for signs. Then he sat down to think until he figured out which way to go. This is what he did now, while my parents sat silently waiting for guidance, with Father fingering his pocket compass.

Regan got them back onto the trail but four miles out from Norway House one side of the cariole broke. This added to Mother's discomfort on what little was left of the hay mattress. The toboggan limped onward and finally reached its destination at 4 a.m. on Sunday, Jan. 20. The night duty nurse opened the door of the hospital and let them in. Seeing Mother's condition, she listened for the fetus's heartbeat and it came through loud and strong. The baby had ridden comfortably and well-protected in its caul. Mother and Father were dead beat and too strung up to sleep but immensely relieved. Father was exhausted, having walked most of the way; Mother was severely constipated but otherwise in the pink of condition. Regan was fine. Poor, scruffy-looking little Tommy, a genuine hero in disguise, was almost played out. Later that morning, Father went to church and Mother wrote home.

For five days they had been practical people preoccupied by anxiety but now the truth sank in on Mother and Father. They were immersed in ecstasy, at least as far as their natures would allow! The sparkling heavens, the white snow blanketing the earth, the silent vastness and the bowing trees transformed the whole universe into an awesome cathedral. Like Christmas actors in the pageant of spiritual birth, they had thought only of getting to the place where the child would be born. They had ventured forth, putting themselves in God's care alongside the other most humble and fiercesome creatures. They had prepared for the trip and kept their attitude correct, asking for guidance and proceeding one day at a time. What they had done was true to themselves as egos, not only to others as examples. Mother rode as a queen and Father was in control. She exuded love and attention and soaked up his shower of love in return. She was his lady and he was her knight, a heroine and hero of a great story. This ride bonded them on another level of existence and kept them going for the rest of their lives.

They felt safe and were sure now that everything was going to be all right. But, as a celebration of the birth of their child, their feelings were premature.

16

Hello To a New Life, Goodbye To the Indian Reserve

ather had to get back to work but would return when the baby was due. After a week's rest, he set out with Regan and Tommy again. Moccasin telegrams (notes handed to travelers encountered on the trail) kept Mother informed of his progress. He had a good sleep at Charlie Saunders' on Tuesday, reached Bobbie Chubb's on Friday and expected to be home on Saturday, in plenty of time to get his sermon ready for Sunday.

Father got up Friday morning, anxious to hit the trail, but when he went out to hitch Tommy up he wasn't there. He thought he must have just wandered off and would be waiting for him and Regan, pawing for grass underneath the snow. Bobbie offered to take them as far as his fish cache on his sleigh but the horse was nowhere in sight. In fact, Tommy was far away, free of the cariole at last, heading full tilt for his stable. When the horse galloped into Oxford House all by himself, with no sign of the cariole or human life, the Indians were very upset. The hours passed with still no sign of Father and Regan and the people's concerns grew very grave. They feared the worst. Dulas and Jack organized a search party and were just setting out at 1 a.m., Sunday, when Father and Regan straggled in, exhausted but safe. They had walked the last sixty miles without any provisions. Father took his church services as usual that morning but then came down with a bad cold which lasted for a week. Regan went back to Bobbie's on Tuesday with a dog team to fetch the cariole and luggage.

Mother didn't need hospital care, so she stayed with the Gaudins for two weeks and then with the Gordons. On Saturday, Feb. 23, a few days before her due date, she went for a walk in the morning, felt some discomfort in the afternoon and went over to the hospital in the evening. Dr. Turpel examined her and said all was normal; the baby would not come for a number of hours, probably not until the next morning. The waters had not yet broken. Then he went with his wife to play bridge five miles up the river.

The labor cramps started coming on stronger and closer together as midnight approached. The night-duty nurse sent a messenger up the river to ask the doctor to come quickly. A new life was determined to come out into the light of the world. The nurse reassured Mother by telling her the severe pains were necessary and instructed her gently in what to do. As the fetus began to emerge, the nurse took one look at it and exclaimed, "What on earth is this?" Mother wondered, "What indeed?" as the nurse turned around and fled. Since this was a real emergency, Mother's nerves held steady as a rock as she waited alone.

Like the hero of Charles Dickens's David Copperfield, the baby was being born in its caul. The unruptured sac of inner membranes was still covering her head and face, making them look grotesque. In English folklore, a child born in this rare manner was destined never to meet death by drowning. David Copperfield's dried-up caul was sold at auction as a good-luck charm. Head Nurse Oliver was awakened from her sleep in another room of the Norway House Hospital and now assumed control. She knew she must break open the caul immediately so the baby would not choke on amniotic fluid with its first breath. And so it was that Tanis Elizabeth Kell, a beautiful, healthy, 7 1/2 lb. baby girl, was born. She was three-quarters of an hour old when the doctor arrived and three days old when Father saw her for the first time. To honor the setting of her nativity, my parents took her name from the Cree word netanis, meaning my daughter.

Father stayed to celebrate Mother's 29th birthday on

March 9th and then they parted again, since it was too cold to take the baby on a trip. They would meet again in seven weeks' time when the spring waters flowed. While Mother and Tanis stayed with the Gordons and Gaudins, Father returned to work. He completed an essay on The Social Development of the Cree and wrote four pamphlets entitled Why We Are Protestants, How to Read the Bible, The Christian Life, and What Jesus Means to Me, all of which the McIvors translated into Cree.

In late May, Father and two guides set out from Oxford House for Norway House with a canoe tied onto a toboggan. The lake-ice was barely thick enough to walk on and the edge-water was barely wide enough to paddle in. They reached Hairy Lake in six days' time, on a Sunday, and found all sorts of campers sitting out in the sun. They looked like a congregation to Father, who had made a vow never to miss church on Sunday if at all possible, so he held a service.

After Father was reunited with Mother and Tanis, they got on a private motor boat that would get them to Warren Landing in time for the Wolverine's first run of the season. They were lucky they didn't drown. The boat was overloaded, almost ran out of gas and leaked so badly all the passengers had to help bail it out. After the annual church conference in Winnipeg ended, they made their way home through oppressive heat and thunder storms. My parents and Tanis reached the Oxford House Reserve at 7 a.m. on June 28, 1929, to begin Father's fifth year of full-time work with the Indians.

Mother fitted the women and girls with winter coats from bales of clothing sent up by congregations in the south and taught them how to handle money through a sale of the left-overs. By charging five cents for each item, they made $5 to help buy siding for the church. (The Indians paid one-tenth of the cost of the mission, excluding Father's salary.)

Eva, the housekeeper, was keen to marry off her fifteen-year-old daughter to a boy who wanted her but Mother persuaded Father to try to get the groom to postpone his plans for a year. However, Eva asserted traditional Cree parental authority and Father had to marry them. Mother tried to tolerate Eva's ways but, when she put Father's white shirts on to boil with his red socks, she replaced her. One day the three cows got out when Father wasn't home so Mother ran a mile-and-a-half to get Fred Stevens, the young teacher from Toronto who had replaced Jack Gordon. Fred dismissed his class and rounded up the cows.

Ten horses working for Ross Navigation Company came in from Cross Lake, pulling ten flat sleighs loaded with drums of gasoline. This was enough to power every canoe in God's Lake and Oxford House and make the silent, skillful paddle a thing of the past. The north was changing forever. A privately-owned Sikorsky, containing a business group headed for York Factory, was forced down on the reserve by the weather. On August 23rd Mother gave breakfast to two NAME (a mining company) pilots, Val Patriarch and Carl Mews, and watched them fly off towards God's Lake. At dusk Val's plane returned but Carl's did not. A search party went out and, after six days, found his plane and a note saying he was walking to Oxford House and expected to arrive in three days' time. Two expert native guides, Donald Wood and Stanley Nattaway, were flown out to track him and, after nine days, narrowed the search down to within a few miles. They found Carl on September 9th, thin and with his clothes all torn by bushes but otherwise unhurt. Donald and Stanley were heroes.

Freeze-up came late, in mid-November, and silence replaced the drone of boat or plane. Since her courageous cariole trek of the previous winter, Mother had acquired a thermometer, parenthood and experience. The idea of other people going out and taking chances scared her stiff. One day, when it was −45 degrees, she got a note from Fred saying he had sent his dog team and toboggan on ahead and was walking the last day in from Cross Lake. He was unfamiliar with the trail but wanted to have an adventure. By the time he arrived, just before midnight, Mother was completely frazzled. Another day she was expecting Bobbie Chubb, now student minister at God's Lake, but he didn't show up. Later she learned he had had to turn back because two of his dogs died.

The day after Christmas, Father and Isaac set out for God's Lake so they could help Bobbie with the New Year's Communion and watchnight services but they hit the wrong trail and wasted two days so had to come back. They started out again and Mother panicked that night when she realized they were camping out at -52 degrees. Actually, Father was reading Readers' Digest by the light of his flashlight because he couldn't sleep and he got a bad frost-bite. Mother hadn't come to this continent just to be widowed and left alone. When he got back she told him he'd better stop taking such risks!

The Indian mothers constantly fondled, hugged and kissed their babies on the mouth and Mother was afraid they were giving them TB. She didn't want Tanis to get it so she kept her in her carriage, except when they were alone, and told the Indians this was the white people's custom. Tanis loved to be entertained by the older children who leaned over to amuse her. If she cried in church, Father stepped down from the pulpit to give her his gold fountain pen to play with in her carriage. On her first birthday, Mother gave a party for all the babies born on the reserve that year. She baked a cake, took pictures and held a contest for the finest Oxford House baby. The Chief was the judge and he chose his grandson. Tanis was adventuresome and in a single day upset her carriage, pulled a lemon pie over her head and swallowed an aspirin. Mother took the hint, let her out and kept her eye on her as she crawled about freely. Now that she was no longer a captive she soon learned to walk.

On February 28th, the Roman Catholic school at Cross Lake burned down because a stove over-heated, killing eight Indian children and the Mother Superior. This tragedy left an aura of dark suspiciousness. Many Indians believed that someone who wanted this to happen had cast a spell upon them but Father was trying to eradicate such superstition.

The hunt was lean and some of the mighty hunters sat brooding, wondering why they were failing, immobilized by depression. On March 10th, Donald Wood, last September's hero, was pulled in from winter camp completely out of his mind. His friends said he had drunk lemon extract two days before but Father suspected something worse. There was no beer on the reserve in this prohibition era but there was home brew. He confirmed the symptoms of gasoline-poisoning in his medical book. There was no antidote and the only cure was to vomit the gasoline up instantly. However, given the time that had elapsed since Donald's drink had been spiked, either by pranksters or himself, he was doomed. Within a few weeks he would develop pneumonia and die horribly. Father thought he should be taken out to hospital by dog team and Mrs. Davidson offered to supply rations for the trip. Father tried to get at the truth of what had happened but, even though the Chief called a meeting, no one talked.

The first mercy flight in northern Manitoba had been flown the previous August, when a wounded Indian was evacuated from Rat's Lake to The Pas, a distance of four hundred and fifty miles. Now the Chief wanted to send out for an airplane for Donald. Father said that would take longer than if they took him out by toboggan and the weather conditions were excellent for dog team travel. The assembled council of Indians then asked Father to administer Communion to Donald. Father knew an Indian with traditional beliefs got better only when he took something which he was convinced would make him better but he was not going to pretend that Communion was like magic. His practical interpretation of the Sacrament of the Lord's Supper was that a community of believers ate bread and drank wine as symbols of their commitment to live out Christ's compassion in their own lives.

A cover-up darkened this tragedy so Father preached on The Sin of Lying. The next day, three guilt-ridden friends of Donald asked if they could haul and chop wood for the school. Father visited Donald every day to pray and provide comfort for him but he was too terrorized by wetigoes. Then Father preached on Elijah, who put the prophets of superstition to death. Since he didn't want the Indians to think he was scolding, he followed up with *For the Lord reproves him whom he loves as a father the son in whom he delights*. Finally, he chose the text *Work out your own salvation*. He wanted the Indians to train their own leaders and not be dependent on white men, like himself, who came and went.

Building lumber arrived, which the people had bought with $100 raised over three years, and Easter was celebrated with spring in the air. Then came a big snow storm, cold weather and corpses from the winter camps. Maggie Wemisk's baby who had been at Tanis's birthday party was one of them. After holding all the funerals and burials, including Donald's, Father donned his old clothes and went out to haul and chop wood.

My parents had decided an Indian reserve was not the best place to raise a family so at the end of the winter Mother began to pack, leaving all she could for the Indians. Father planted separate gardens for the Chief, Isaac, the horses and cows, the school and the whole community. Tanis, trying to help, toddled along behind him and picked up the seeds he dropped. As farewell gifts, Alice presented a birchbark sewing basket, three birchbark trivets and a mosquito-proof travel outfit for Tanis. She made it from Mother's left-over curtain material; it had elastic around the wrists and ankles and a wide, stiff-brimmed hat. This was covered with netting that could be tied with a ribbon around the waist so Tanis could play with a small toy inside it. At mealtimes, when the camp-fire smoke kept the mosquitoes away, she could take the hat off.

As she motored off on June 15th, 1930, Mother knew she could never forget this little band of Indians. They were standing and singing, "In the sweet bye and bye, we shall meet on that beautiful shore." "Oxford House" (not "Tomato Soup") was etched indelibly across Mother's heart.

Seventy years later, Tanis saw a picture of herself crying in fright at her first sight of a white child and understood how traumatic it had been for her to leave the Indian reserve.

Part III

The Third Child Seeks To Outfox Her Perceived Destiny

Thistletown Backyard, 1947

17

The Thirties, a World War, a Deep Trust and Family Moves

My parents were posted to Nakina, a northwestern Ontario railway town of six hundred people who depended completely on each other for entertainment. No one owned a car and the only road out of town led to a local lake. Two weeks after the move, Mother took Tanis to England for the summer where she met a lot of relatives. When she came home, she called Father "Uncle Daddy."

Mother stood out in Nakina because of her English accent and vocabulary. She trod (not stepped) on the ground, she sewed with reels of cotton, rather than spools of thread, and she got water out of a bucket, not a pail. She played a few games of tennis before winter set in and made friends with her neighbor, Mrs. Chalmers, who had a two-year-old child.

The United Church had no building and the Anglicans no minister (the one from Hearst came down every second weekend) so they co-operated. Father rented the church or else used the school for services and meetings. Every second weekend he preached at Armstrong, one hundred and thirteen miles up the line, leaving on Friday and hopping off the freight train to visit parishioners along the way. When she was alone with Mother, Tanis remembers peering through the cracks in the shed to look at the men who rode the rail. Mother told them to wait there while she made them a sandwich.

On Mar. 2, 1931, my sister Enid Mary, a good-natured baby who kept everyone in a jolly mood, was born in the Nakina Hospital. Tanis sensed that Enid was Father's girl. There was now a little less room for her on his knee.

The prospect of moving south to the three-point rural charge of Lemonville, Bloomington and Ballantrye, where they would have a car and be able to visit Father's family, excited Mother. But the reality turned out to be miserable. The Lemonville parsonage had no furnace, the car radiator froze leaving them stranded on a trip into Toronto and the work was hard. Six Protestant churches were competing for the faithful in a district with three one-room schools. Mother had her hands full after I arrived. Just because she was setting a good example didn't mean she never got jealous. She put her foot down and insisted that Father always be home for a cup of tea with her at 10 a.m., 4 p.m. and 10 p.m. She didn't want to have gossip arising from his visiting ladies of the congregation socially or at odd hours. Tea became a lifetime ritual for them.

My parents decided not to have any more children but to thank God they had three fine, healthy, ones. Earlier Father had thought big families were the happiest and Mother's ideal had been to have four children, two of each sex. When we moved right into the city in 1934 Mother was expected to be happier.

When I was a teen-ager, Mother used to say that whenever life got so tough she couldn't stand it something happened that made things take a turn for the better. When I was five, I saw her crying and begging for forgiveness on her knees at the feet of Grandma at the farm. Her offense was that she had ordered two dresses from Eaton's catalogue, one to wear in the house and one for Sundays. Grandma accused her of being extravagant—she could have worn an old dress at home and sewn her own for Sunday best. Poor Mother couldn't stand up to such scrutiny and her nerves fell to pieces.

Then things improved. The doctor discovered she was anemic and gave her iron pills to combat the condition. Cousin Mary came to live with us while attending Normal School. We started going as a family to the occasional movie such as

The Wizard of Oz, Fantasia, Dumbo and The Great Dictator. Mother's favorite was One Foot in Heaven, the story of a minister's wife. We attended classical concerts at a synagogue and a Catholic church. At a bazaar at the Church of All Nations, she bought my sisters embroidered, Hungarian drawstring blouses which, luckily for me, they would some day outgrow. We were invited to other ministers' homes and to missionaries' picnics at High Park where we fed the dromedary. In summers, we traded houses with the ministers in Sundridge and Powassan and played with boys' toys, which were more interesting than girls'.

One sunny morning in late August, 1939, Father lifted his head from the radio and said "This is the darkest day in the history of the British Empire." World War II had broken out. Mother started knitting socks for soldiers out of wool given her by the Red Cross and sent parcels to her family, who were caught in the Blitz. She was worried to death about them and offered to take our cousins, David and Janet. It was too dangerous for them to cross the ocean so they were evacuated to the English countryside instead.

Grandma Kell died this year but I don't remember her funeral. After Grandpa and Uncles Wilson and Clifton died, Grandma had put on a black dress and taken to her rocking chair. She showed little interest in anything, certainly not me, during our dutiful visits to Cookstown. Father was always looking for an expression of approval from her. He felt very responsible, being the only one of her four men left. Aunt Mabel inherited the family estate and then she married a wealthy widower, Frank Fidler, at age fifty. When she died in 1965, she left her money to my sisters and me and our three first cousins, Albert Kell, Mary Kell and John Goodfellow.

My first-grade teacher, Jeannie McDowell, had been in Paris in early Summer, 1939, and must have been talking to members of the underground in the cafés. Otherwise, I can't explain how she knew to tell us that the Germans were herding Jewish people into concentration camps, killing them, burning their bodies and making them into soap. I did not pass on this unbelievable scoop to my parents or sisters or anyone. I just felt wiser in my heart. It was a trust and made a very deep impression on me. Miss McDowell also taught us to sing O Canada in both English and French and to sing La Marseillaise. I liked her; she put me on the grade two side of the classroom.

In 1940, we moved up the hill to the new parsonage on Dufferin Street, in between our church and the Parsons' farm. "C.B." and his wife were rich members of our congregation who invited us for dinner and let us toboggan on their hill. C.B. lived to be 100 and have a school named after him. Our school friends, Ida and Linda Gambin (changed from Gambino), invited Enid and me to a party in their restaurant and taught us how to twirl spaghetti on a spoon. My father, being less of a financial success, sold his building lots at the corner of Yonge and Steeles streets because of the high taxes.

On the other side of Dufferin Street from our house was the school we attended, Briar Hill Public. There would be no more falling and scraping of knees on the cinder path up to school and no more considering of buttercups and dandelions (a poor substitute for *lilies of the field*) along the way. By now, I had a fairly well developed idea of the man I would marry. He would be as sturdy and cuddly as a teddy bear, have a nice smile like Grandfather Ward, be as exotic and elegant as an embroidered Hungarian drawstring blouse and be wise enough in his heart not to make comments about Jews.

One day soon after moving, we got the terrible news that Uncle Joe, Captain Joseph Burnett, was dead. His Australian cruiser, The Sydney, was blown up by the enemy in the Japan Sea and went down with him standing on the bridge and all hands on board. Cousins Patrick, Rory and Bridget now had no father and Aunt Enid no husband. A Toronto Star reporter came to our house to interview Mother, who gave him a picture of Uncle Joe in uniform. In our diningroom she hung a picture of him in his rugby stripes.

Father did not enlist because he was over forty years old and had received a service medal in World War I. Besides, something was wrong with him. He was gargling loudly in the bathroom each morning, sitting for an hour a day in front of a sun lamp, drinking carrot juice and at times fasting. Mother was being sympathetic to him so we knew something was up. She persuaded him to go to see a doctor who was also a good psychologist. Father had been at Fairbank for seven years and his storehouse of ideas for sermons was running low. Every Sunday morning and evening when he rose in the pulpit to face the congregation, he not only got butterflies in his stomach, he got a cramp in his intestines. The doctor diagnosed his problem as a spastic colon and suggested the best medicine would be for him to make a complete change.

The Fairbank congregation gave us a farewell party and we packed up and headed for Cochrane, five hundred miles straight up Yonge Street, in the summer of '42. Father had "preached for a call" and been invited to be the minister at St. Paul's United Church. Tanis was ready to enter high school and, according to the results of province-wide examinations, the schools in Cochrane were excellent. We drove through Muskoka, North Bay, Temagami, the Height of Land, the ghost-town of Cobalt, and stayed by the waterfall in Latchford at a friend's home. The next day, we went through Haileybury, New Liskeard, Englehart and saw the guard-tower of the prisoner-of-war camp at Matheson. The trees got smaller and the soil sandier as we traveled through bush, bush, bush, past pot-hole lakes to Porquis Junction and the airstrip at Nellie's Lake.

We three were squeezed into the back while Mother sat in front with her feet in the dishpan, reading a historical novel and knitting rapidly. Every year she made a pullover for each of us and a cardigan for Father, if he needed one, but she never knitted herself a sweater. She gave him candies from the glove compartment to suck on and told him to get his eyes back on the road if he looked sideways or twisted his head around to say a word to us. We only went off into the ditch once. As we neared our destination, our excitement mounted and so did Mother's agitation.

As we got closer and closer to our new home, Mother wailed, "We never should have come here. Now what are you expecting of me?" By the time our eyes read the sign "Cochrane, Population 3,000," a full-fledged panic attack was ringing in our ears. For every fear and objection, Father had a reassurance. He reminded her that she had visited here before and liked it. He had checked out the house and the people and they were of the finest caliber. They would like her; and Ethel Wilkinson, the girls' schoolteacher, had promised to come up for a visit. The girls were growing up and would help and be good company, "Won't you, girls?" Father's head swiveled around again and Mother told him to watch where he was going. I wasn't too happy but I was secure. They were a team.

We drove back to Stroud to spend July on Aunt Clara's farm, a pretty place with whitewashed stones and flower beds bordering the curved driveway from the house to the barn. Uncle Roy Goodfellow was superintendent of the Sunday School we attended at Stroud United Church. At the annual Kell family picnic, we got introduced to and raced against second-, third- and once-removed cousins we hadn't even known existed. Most of them were farmers and one family characteristic was a slow heart beat. We were all descended from William and Mary Kell who had immigrated in 1850 and given birth to Thomas, Elizabeth, John, William and Mary. Father reminded everyone how lucky we were to have our Methodist heritage. Underneath, we were all the same kind of nice people, preoccupied with striving to save our souls.

We also went to the Campbell reunion at a site on the shore of Lake Simcoe where a sign saying "Gentiles only" was posted. The Campbells were dark-haired, healthy, sturdy, musical, funloving farmers. My great-grandfather, Matthew, had marched with his brothers (all Orangemen) to York in 1837 to defend Queen Victoria against the rebel, William Lyon Mackenzie. Grandma, one of eleven, did not go to church as a girl because they were too poor to have nice clothes. They were also very independent.

Every day on Aunt Clara's farm, we woke to the rooster's crowing and the cows' mooing. We fed the pigs and chickens, collected the eggs, played in the hay loft, ate wheat kernels out of a bin, learned to drive a team of horses, walked down the lane to get the mail, picked beans, peas, corn, plums and cherries, took a drink to the men who were haying in the fields, fetched the cows from pasture and helped milk them. Aunt Clara showed us how to wash a separator, examine eggs over a light bulb to see if they had blood spots, pull out pin feathers and clean a freshly killed chicken. As a treat for us, she made ice cream with her own cream and maple syrup. Sometimes we walked barefoot to Mrs. Goodfellow's cottage on Lake Simcoe to have a swim.

On rainy days, we played the player piano which was stocked with rolls of popular classics, such as In a Monastery Garden and Indian Love Song. Once, we went to Collingwood to see the shipbuilding yard and jam factory. Farmers never went to the store for food but, if a machine part broke, the men had to go into Barrie to get it fixed. While they were busy doing that, we women looked around the hardware store. The display of china and the pretty paper serviettes were my first art gallery.

None of these activities was Mother's cup of tea, except the trips into town, so she was always wrought up, miserable and irritable when we were at the farm. While Father was out in the fields doing what he loved doing best, she was inside nursing a migraine headache, working herself up into a state because he didn't have his hat on, or calling us in for a nap when we were having the most fun. I thought he was neglecting her so I asked him, "What's the matter? Don't you love her?" He was shocked and said, "Of course I do." (In fact, he found her hair-do too severe and wished she would wear a pink dress occasionally, instead of always looking like a minister's wife.) It never occurred to me that Mother was intelligent or capable. If anyone tried to give her a compliment she shrugged it off, as if there was something wrong with accepting it. Father tried to get her to practise driving the car around the haystacks but it made her too nervous. She was no fun on the farm; she just came there to preserve the family pattern. At least she and Aunt Clara, who had a wonderful sense of humor, got along well.

The Cochrane "manse" (the Presbyterian term for a Methodist "parsonage") had a clear view of Lake Commando, a butterfly-shaped, pot-hole lake with the gap between its two peninsulae spanned by a little bridge. Boardwalks built on stilts fronted the houses and surrounded the lake. A diving tower, wooden booms and strings of buoys were set out in the bay, where all Cochrane children learned how to swim. Main Street was so wide, after having been burned down and rebuilt twice, that a huge snowbank bisected it in the winter. Wartime rationing was in force and some things could be bought only with coupons. Mother sent me uptown with a coupon for laundry powder and I got the only kind I could get, Rinso. A big railway worker with a box of Ivory Snow came up to me and asked if I would trade, since his wife needed a stronger product to get his greasy overalls clean. I wasn't sure it was a good deal but who was I to argue?

During our first year in this half-French, half-allophone ("English") town, Mother was very run down. Her menstrual bleeding scarcely stopped from period to period so she had to have a hysterectomy. On the day of her operation, Father, who had faith that nothing would go wrong as long as we stuck to God's path for us, got an awful shock when they wheeled her out into the hospital corridor on a stretcher. She looked so gray he thought she was dead. The doctor patted him on the shoulder and said "She's just fine." You wouldn't have known it from her delicate nerves but Mother had a robust physique.

Our house looked out on Cochrane High School, located on one peninsula. English high school students walked on the side of the street closest to the lake and French convent students walked on the other. Sometimes a few taunts or stones were thrown. Tanis was walking to school one winter day while Mr. Marwick, the principal, was watching her with his thumb on the electric bell button so she would get there on time. She was just rounding the curve of the lake, when a runaway horse came galloping up behind her. (Delivery trucks and most cars were put up on blocks in the winter.) The horse had gone too close to the edge of the lake and its empty rig jack-knifed and was dangling down the slope. Tanis dived and rolled out of the way but couldn't avoid being hit by the corner of the sleigh. Mr. Marwick thought she had been killed but, luckily, she just suffered a concussion.

Miss Wilkinson came for a visit and she and my parents had fun pretending they were a ménage à trois. They were like the identical-twin Stewart sisters who sat in a pew every Sunday with one man between them. Mother had discovered the secret of how a minister's wife could make friends: you invited someone congenial from your past charge up to visit you on your new one.

Enid became ill with what the doctor diagnosed as a severe case of 'flu, so my parents moved her out of the bed we shared and onto a couch in the diningroom. Our manual training teacher, Louis Tivy, came with a box of chocolates when he heard about her symptoms. She got better after some weeks and back to her active life at school. She was chosen for the girls' hockey team and her boyfriend, Timmy Horton, let her use his hockey stick. She was the envy of all the other girls because Timmy was our star. Our team beat all the out-of-town teams, thanks to Timmy's amazing break-aways down the length of the ice. We cheered him on at the top of our lungs. We all knew Timmy would be an NHL star but never dreamt he would one day give his name to a Canadian icon, Tim Hortons. Enid had met him in grade seven when Miles Horton sat in the desk in front of hers. He told her he didn't like his name and asked her if she would call him Tim instead. She did, and got her friends to do the same. "He was very determined," she recalls. "When the grade ten teacher called him Miles, he wouldn't answer." A few years later, it became apparent that one of Enid's legs was shorter than the other and she had to be fitted for a special shoe. The illness which had attacked her, and had crippled Mr. Tivy's arm and leg when he was a child, was polio.

The brash town of Cochrane, barely twenty years old, was having a rejuvenating effect on my parents. Mother let her hair grow and the hairdresser styled it in a roll that looked attractive underneath the ermine-tail cadet-style hat she had made out of six pelts she had saved. Father took up curling and rode our intermediate-size girls' bicycle to Lady Minto Hospital to visit the Indians in the TB ward and other patients. He formed an association with the other ministers (Catholic, Baptist and Anglican) which met monthly over lunch in a restaurant. He drove to the rural communities of Clute, Hanna and Hunta to preach and sometimes went up to the line to Fraserdale. He trained student ministers from southern Ontario whom my sisters and I found to be very entertaining house guests. Mother went to the dentist's wife's bridge parties (she didn't play), led girls' church groups and volunteered to help keep the town's little library going. She hosted a WMS conference where "pinwheel" sandwiches, made with maraschino cherries, peanut butter and banana, were served. She even let us keep a kitten Father brought home from a potato farm. The cold, dry air and crunchy snow of a -60-degree Cochrane winter must have inspired her good mood.

One day, Mother was riding on a train to a WMS conference in Timmins when a woman from Hearst said, "I heard a funny story about you the other day. You left behind the farewell gift the ladies of Nakina gave you." Quite so! When she was leaving Nakina in 1932 the WA presented Mother with a beautiful set of hand-carved crystal. It consisted of a water pitcher and six matching glasses. One of the glasses was later found to be cracked so her neighbor, Mrs. Chalmers, volunteered to send it back to Ryrie Birks in Toronto to get it replaced. Mother left one of her packing-cases open with the distinctive blue Birks box conspicuously out on top for Mrs. Chalmers's convenience. She would freight the whole thing to Lemonville when my parents knew their new address.

A pair of malevolent eyes passing by the window of the empty house saw the blue box and concluded it had been left behind. In retrospect, Mother realized it may have been unwise of her to demolish the president of the Nakina WA, the local queen, so roundly at tennis.

18

Postwar Growing-up, Conflicted, In Small Towns and the Big City

While Mother's past caught up with her in Cochrane, I reached my adolescent years. I sang in the choir, attended mid-week groups and memorized the Apostles' Creed and the Catechism in preparation for church membership and first Communion. Father's definition of "reverend" was to accept completely the Church's authority, doctrine and procedures. His preaching was more critical, constantly challenging us to do more with our lives.

One day, Inspector Raymond Cassie from the Department of Education came into our classroom and announced he was going to give us a test. He said we would not be able to finish it but we should just do our best. I must have been dying to be challenged because, with face flushing and heart racing, I accomplished the impossible. Next day, Mr. Cassie came back into our classroom and said he was going to choose just one person, the person who smiled the best, to do another test. I not only smiled, I blushed. He took me alone to a small, upstairs room but that was no fun. As soon as I finished one problem, he gave me a harder one. When he eventually asked me to copy a line diagram while looking at my hands through a mirror, I started to cry out of frustration. He told me I was too conscientious, which made me cry even more. (Why couldn't he have said, "You're a bright girl. You've done a good job?") It was eerie to hear him say I was working at the grade ten level. I was just glad to get back where I belonged, in grade eight, and hear no more about tests.

At the Roman Catholic convent where I took piano and theory lessons, the naked crucifixes on the walls and the pallid statues made me uneasy. I can still feel the nun clamping her hand over mine, as I played, so I could not move my wrist, only my fingers. She told me my father's church had been founded by a man who had eight wives. The Catholic girls talked about going to confession, eating fish on Fridays and fasting during Lent. They said rosaries and worried about mortal and venal sins and going to hell or purgatory. I was glad Father didn't burden his flock with such fears but I was still nervous. Once I came home to an empty house while my parents were at a funeral. When I went to hang up my coat, the wire hangers in the hall closet started jangling like skeletons in a death dance and wouldn't stop. My terror lasted until someone knocked on the door. It was a woman in a hat who had walked all the way up from the railway station because she needed to go to the bathroom and the one there was closed. I was as relieved to see her as she was to relieve herself.

When everyone was there, the atmosphere of our home was congenial. Mother had good ideas for Halloween costumes and suggested the winning name for our high school dance nights, Kewateens. She liked the magazine, Calling All Girls, and the radio programs, The Happy Gang, The Hit Parade and Hockey Night in Canada. She could give help with homework, piano, sewing, knitting or anything, it seemed. She came to our Kiwanis Music Festivals and school productions of HMS Pinafore and A Midsummer Night's Dream. In short, she was experiencing what it was like to grow up in Canada. We pinned pictures of movie idols on our bedroom walls and went about crooning and dancing. Father remained oblivious in his study, applying the experience he had gained on Indian reserves. (He had learned to preach in spite of dogs howling outside, flies buzzing in the windows, babies crying and crawling, mothers rocking and nursing them and men wandering around who did not realize it was the custom to sit.)

The year 1945 marked the death of President Franklin Delano Roosevelt in April, VE Day in May, my 12th birthday in July and VJ Day in August. We danced and sang on a platform set up in the street outside the Post Office. No more telegrams bringing bad news; no new grieving mothers, fathers, widows, grandparents, children and younger brothers and sisters; no more acting-out in war games; no more sending parcels; no more booklets of war savings stamps; no more rationing; no more posters and paper serviettes with bull dogs on them; no more cadet drills and no more men in nifty uniforms uptown. As well as local sons home on leave, we had Americans who manned the DEW (distant early warning) line. We didn't let the annihilating of Hiroshima and Nagasaki with the world's first atomic bombs spoil our celebrations.

Uncle Eric was now back to civilian life as a solicitor, after having been a squadron leader in the RAF balloon barrage. He wrote to Mother that The Cottage had been sold for a sum of 3,000 pounds and Granny had moved into a flat. She had loaned him the money to purchase a three-hundred-year-old house and the interest he paid her covered her rent. The bakery, which had expanded all over the country, had been sold to Garfield Weston but the shares were tied up in a fund to support the widows of the partners.

I walked, whistling, with my skates slung over my shoulder, to the Cochrane arena, picking my way through splotches of urine, snot, sputum and vomit. It was invigorating to be out from under parental control! I inhaled fumes of cheap whiskey around the corner drinking-houses, each with a Ladies Entrance on the side, but I never saw a lady. The clientele were bushwhackers in plaid jackets who came off the Polar Bear Express from Moosonee. I was afraid of being accosted by a man but the ones emerging from the hotels weren't capable of much more than staggering and passing out in snowbanks.

Sometimes I asked myself Why am I here? Where am I going? What are we doing? What sense lies in a bunch of specks whirling around on a ball in space? When I walked alone, my head spun. One day an inner voice piped up, "I'm going to make something out of me," and I marched all the way home to that rhythm. My best friend, Eleanor Dobenko, had lived in Cochrane all her life and knew lots of exciting things to do. One day we met some boys who were doing target practice in the bush with a twelve-gauge shotgun and they let us have a turn.

The day of my first menstrual period, I took a shortcut over a corner of the lake during the spring thaw and barely managed to keep myself afloat on floes that had sunk beneath the surface of the water. That summer, Eleanor and I went for a hike near the 100'-high forestry tower and then accidentally started a fire while trying to roast wieners for a picnic. We ran through the flames in the dry field like crazy, flapping our blanket and jackets over them, until we put them out.

You might think that a minister's daughter who was a pillar of the church on Sundays would behave in an exemplary way throughout the rest of the week but this was not always so. I stole the padlock from the golf course gate, cheated a customer on my Timmins Press paper route, took out a street light by throwing a stone at it and smashed a girlfriend's bike without owning up to it. I did not always understand what was happening to me. I even joined a mob I happened to fall in with by accident outside the Post Office. A bunch of kids were pushing the sled of a French Canadian girl and her little brother back down the icy hill to the lake every time they got to the top. I can't forget the look of hurt, dignified determination in her eyes.

One of the most bizarre incidents that happened to me was that I filled my pants (sensible bloomers with elastic around the leg-holes) in church. I brazenly kept on posing in the sun's rays reflected through the stained-glass window, as if someone else was making the stench. When we got out into the fresh air, I noisily commented about the smell to my friends and pointed at another girl who was hurrying home. Everyone was fooled, except Mother. I buried the dirty underpants at the back of my clothes cupboard and, when she found them, she confronted me. Then she just turned around and went off to clean up my mess without any reproof.

One night, two boys serenaded me from the street below my bedroom window but this romance lasted only until they found other girls who knew something about sex, which I did not. Another night, when I came in late from roaming around with my gang, Mother accused me of being a "hussy," a word I had never heard before. We had just been going about feeling good about ourselves and had snuck into the railway roundhouse to explore.

The topsy-turviness subsided without my delinquent deeds ever being exposed. I would have died. Thank God, I was able to preserve the image of being a good person in my own eyes as well as others'. I got away from my sneaky side and became an honest person, stealing cookies from the pantry excepted. A few years later, I recognized the picture of a criminal emblazoned on the front pages of the Toronto newspapers. He was Steve Suchan of the notorious Boyd gang who had been captured and sentenced to death for shooting a policeman. To me he was Val Lesso, the big fifteen-year-old with sensitive eyes and empty hands who sat squeezed into a desk at the back of our grade-ten classroom. He had been brought in from the bush because he had never had a chance to attend school. Now he was supposed to catch on to the idea of it by observing us normal kids. I guess he finally found some friends but they were not good ones and I felt very sorry.

Tanis did her job well and graduated from high school with nine firsts (75% plus) and two seconds (66-74%) on the "departmentals." Only nine subjects were needed for university admission. Her best friend, Adrienne Duranceau, the judge's daughter, achieved thirteen firsts. No doubt about it; it was time for our family to move back to within commuting distance of Victoria College.

A call came for Father from Thistletown, Ontario, thirteen miles from Toronto City Hall, where we took up residence in 1947. Our house stood at a fork in the Weston Road, where a black-and-white signpost offered a choice of Malton, Weston or Woodbridge. The general store was caricatured by Gregory Clark and Jimmy Frise in their newspaper cartoon, Birdseye

Centre. At the back of our house, the narrow yard sloped to the Humber River bed, an open range where the trickle swelled to a flow only in spring. In summer and fall, we collected tiny fossils embedded in rock and pieces of iridescent shale. (On Oct. 15, 1954, this waterway was flooded so badly during Hurricane Hazel that, when the water receded, a car was left stuck in the limbs of a tree.)

Thistletown United Church was the hub of the pre-television social life of this partly rural, partly suburban community and three healthy, long-haired, good-looking girls, eighteen, sixteen and fourteen years of age, were a welcome addition to it. The old town hall was available for amateur theater productions and community dancing where persons of all ages stomped and swung vigorously through routines such as The Grand Old Duke of York. We invited school friends and church groups to our home for wiener, corn or marshmallow roasts by the river, complete with singsongs and smooching on plaid car rugs underneath the moon and stars.

Although she was ready to return to the south, being uprooted again agitated my menopausal mother. She was anxious about whether she would ever see Granny again, anxious about saving for retirement, anxious about not owning her own house or furniture, anxious about the wrinkles in her neck, anxious about money for our clothes and education, anxious about whether Tanis was going to have a nervous breakdown at age nineteen, anxious about her anxiousness. Her mind started racing, running on faster and faster without her being able to stop it. She could not tolerate being in a car going more than forty miles per hour. When her birthday came, I had $5 to spend on a present and saw a blue dress on sale for that price. I bought it and she wore it to a meeting the very next day.

With money accumulated from Father's wedding fees, Mother bought herself a New Look suit, with the hemline several inches below the knee, and a plane ticket to England. Uncle Eric met her in the middle of the night so she did not see the ruins of Portsmouth until the next morning. Wesley Chapel was gone and so was the Guildhall. Granny had become a chain smoker and tea-drinker during the war and had little to do in her flat except crossword puzzles. As Mother faced the prospect of spending three months with her, her nervous condition worsened. She could not sleep and felt so upset and depressed she had to go to the doctor and get pills for her glands and nerves. She tried to relive old pleasures, walking around Portsmouth and London and going to the theater, but felt unneeded, homesick and out of place. Her New Look was an affront to people reeling from five years of devastation and deprivation.

In order to avert a nervous breakdown, Mother phoned to say she was flying home early. Father met her in Montreal and they drove the rest of the night along the shore of the St. Lawrence River. The doctor in Thistletown prescribed sodium amytol (a barbiturate she was to remain on for the next forty-two years) and advised her to find a hobby. Just at this time, Alice McIvor from Oxford House sent the three of us deerskin brooches she had made. With a new friend, Mother enrolled in a night class in leatherwork at Weston Collegiate and liked it so much she took a second course. She found a level of peacefulness in tooling, carving and dyeing handbags, wallets, belts, desk sets and jewelry out of soft leather.

However, the atmosphere of our home was still stifled by her nerves. She could not stand the tension of an argument or a decision left hanging so discussions around the dinner table had to be cut off. No one was allowed to beat Mother at Scrabble, the only table game she played. "Family fun" consisted of Father playing a game with us while Mother read a book. Christmas Day with family became an excruciating bore, except when my sisters and I invited our own friends.

Our parents encouraged the free expression of emotions so no one's frustrations stayed pent up. We posted a schedule for dish-washing duties but still threw wet dishrags and cracked tea towels at each other. Once I stomped out of the house in a fury, slammed the door and walked around in the pouring rain without a coat for twenty minutes. When I came back, The Examples were sitting in the livingroom, reading, as if nothing had happened.

One day someone knocked urgently on our front door and a hysterical woman burst in yelling "Is there a God? Is there a God?" Father assured her that there was. I think he put his arm around her shoulder, although it was very unusual for him to be demonstrative. We got her seated on the chesterfield and Mother soon produced tea and a plateful of cookies. Father found the woman's husband outside looking for her; he brought him in and the three of them talked until she settled down and the couple went off hand in hand.

My sisters and I led a double social life, one connected with school and the other with the church. Father didn't seem to care whether I married one of the junior farmers I square-danced with at Ebenezer or Sharon (the two other points on the charge) or one of the boys I met at school, just so long as I got an education. Mother told us to go out with a lot of different boys and do interesting things. She did not believe there was just one man for every woman but a certain type of man. In a rare moment of self-revelation, she showed us the long, white, kid gloves she had worn to gala balls, and her dance cards with a partner's signature opposite each number. The important name was the last one, for the home waltz. I couldn't believe Mother had once had a life of her own.

Sunday was our day of rest so I always did my homework and cramming for exams a day early. In health class, our teacher told us it is important to have a philosophy of life and this worried me because I had no idea what I really believed. One thing my friends found hard to understand, and I did too, was that our family drank no alcohol. My parents also did not believe in gambling or tipping but those things were not such a social blot on me. As a child, I had signed "the pledge" on a day in church when the Temperance Society handed out tiny yellow pencils and cards to sign. We promised never to touch a drop of alcohol. Father said he was "setting a good example for others" by not drinking. He was proud to have resisted the temptations offered by the pubs and prostitutes in the harbor when he was a sailor. He had even turned down his rum ration on board ship.

Our family had a history of alcohol addiction. My great-grandfather, Matthew Campbell, succumbed to it and so did one of his sons, Jim. The word-of-mouth story goes that Matthew left great-grandmother and their infant son outside in the cold in a cutter because he had to go into the hotel and get a drink and the boy died soon after. Jim squandered the family farm so that great-grandmother was left destitute. Grandma had to take her in when my Father was a child and support her for the rest of her life. Small wonder Grandma was such a tee-totaler that "the wets" teased her by throwing empty whiskey bottles into the lane. She picked them up and filled them with her home-made chili sauce. On Mother's side, my great-grandmother Ward was an alcoholic.

Atop the social ladder at Weston Collegiate and Vocational School were the Eaton's and Simpsons reps. Two chosen individuals, a girl and a boy, represented these stores. They sponsored semi-formal dances which were the highlight of the social year for Toronto-area students. The High Holiday Hop, The Bunny Hop and The Cinderella Ball rocked the Royal York or King Edward Hotels under the batons of Tommy Dorsey and Bobby Gimby, the music of Glen Miller and the crooning of the Mills Brothers and the Ink Spots. One year my boyfriend, the Simpsons rep, arrived in a car that had a rumble seat. I was hard-pressed to squeeze my crinoline and long taffeta dress into it, all the while shielding my white camellia corsage to keep it from turning brown.

Each school had its own personality, fostered through football rivalry, and I was particularly intimidated by the Lawrence Park girls who were so confident, chic and cliquish. Weston suited me because it was ninety years old and had academic traditions and school uniforms. But something about me seemed different. Other kids told me I had been brought up in a shell and had better learn to stick up for myself or else I'd get walked over. Little did I realize how right they were. I was operating priggishly under my childish ideas that money and fame were of no importance and the way to become first was to be last. On the outside I was happy and confident but inside I was becoming morbidly self-conscious.

The United Nations Declaration of Human Rights was passed and I feared Father's ideal Christian commonwealth would be doomed in the clamor for individual rights. He thought the Declaration was an advancement for humankind and so did my idol, Eleanor Roosevelt, so I fell into line. Up until then we were accustomed to asking what was good for God, Church and Country. It was a time of big changes. We first watched television by standing on the sidewalk outside an electronics store and viewing a set in the window. At one of the big dances, we recorded our voices on vinyl, a new technology. I thought society was going to the dogs when people started borrowing instead of saving up the money before buying something.

Being so good at setting an example, I naturally tried out for and landed the lead role in the school play two years running. Then I won the prize for Personality, Leadership and Co-operation in my final year. But these things were a sham; my ego was running on empty inside. When Mother noticed my weeping in church, she sent me to see her doctor who found nothing wrong, except that I was a little depressed, and gave me three sodium amytol pills to take if needed.

On weekends, my friends and I went on foursomes to movies and then to one of our parents' homes afterwards. The code of virginity was strong in those pre-birth-control-pill days. My girlfriends and I would sooner have died than got pregnant. I felt wishy-washy and vague, with no idea of who I was or what I should do, so in the summer holidays I copied my sisters. I went to work as a kitchen girl at a children's camp owned by our parents' best friends, Steven and Beatrice Mathers. He was a classmate of Father's at theological college. I forgot a lot of my troubles in this beautiful cottage country where the kitchen boy took me canoeing, we played fool's bridge and saw movies in Parry Sound.

When I graduated from high school as winner of the Victoria College Class of '29 prize for proficiency in languages, I applied the $200 award to my fees as a student of Social & Philosophical Studies at the University of Toronto. People assumed I was an OK girl, continuing in my family's tradition.

19

A Motto of Truth Saves the Day In My Dire Crises of Ego And Soul

In the fall of 1950 I started university, getting myself nominated as class representative on the Student Administrative Council and then wondering "What for?" I commuted for ninety minutes from Thistletown and ate lunch out of a brown-paper bag on the carpet of Wymilwood with other students of "Soc. & Phil." When we discovered that none of us had a date for the fall dance, we held a hen party instead. Those Women Without Men are still my best friends today. The next summer, I supervised a city playground along with a high school student, Morley Safer, who is now a host of the CBS program 60 Minutes.

I took my parents up on their offer of "one year in residence" in my second year, switched to English Language & Literature and settled into a ground-floor room in an ivy-clad house on Bloor Street with street cars rattling by. It was demolished in the sixties to make room for the Colonnade, a shopping-center/apartment complex. We twelve residents took turns on phone duty and gobbled up coffee dates at the Chez Paree, Honey Dew and Murrays after studying. Football weekends to Queens, Western and McGill, plays, semi-formal dances, Sunday teas and parties with the boys from Burwash Hall kept us busy. Men were allowed to visit in the common room but they had to leave by 10 p.m. One couple stayed necking night after night with his heel in the door so that, technically speaking, he wasn't inside. In the summer, I worked in a dark room at Kodak for $54 a week plus overtime, punching numbers into rolls of undeveloped film. I felt abandoned when my family left on vacation and I had to go home to an empty house.

The Thistletown congregation feted my parents on their twenty-fifth wedding anniversary by presenting them with an engraved silver tea service. It was a church-basement occasion designed to celebrate a working partnership. Mother gloried in wearing a corsage and pouring tea. Father drank tea and tittered with the women of the WA who all loved him and envied his wife. When the people found out that Mother had received a telegram two days before informing her that Granny had died of a stroke, they were impressed with the way she had set aside her feelings so as not to spoil the party.

Granny died with only forty-six pounds in her bank account, not enough to honor her bequest of twenty-five pounds to each grandchild upon turning twenty-one. Uncle Eric wanted to do so on her behalf but his house's value had plummeted and his debts risen. Grandfather had taken too much money out of the bakery to pay for his children's education and clothes so Uncle Eric had had to pay off his debt and keep the business afloat. He wrote to Mother, asking her to lend him two hundred and fifty pounds out of her share of nine hundred. She interrupted her carping at Father about money to reply, "Take three hundred and feel free to borrow against the rest." When she received five hundred pounds, the maximum the government allowed out at once, she bought some small pieces of furniture. She guarded the rest jealously, even though Father always said he had "more money than I know what to do with." She said that was because he expected her to retire in an old school bus.

Mother had always suggested I might want to take a year out of school, since I had skipped twice, and I took her advice after a crisis arose during my third year. I was nineteen years old and so depressed that I walked out of a drug store without picking up my change and stepped off the curb onto busy St. George Street without looking to see if any cars were coming. A car squealed to a halt and the driver yelled and tooted at me. I was shocked to think I had almost committed suicide.

Realizing I needed help, I went to see the Dean of Women at Victoria College, Dr. Jessie Macpherson, who was famous for her lectures on sex. (She started the series by saying an atmosphere of freedom was necessary; you began by freeing yourself of all your clothes.) She told me that in cases such as mine she often found that something in the family was the source of the trouble. This was a helpful comment but I didn't want to confide in her. Father had taken her skating when they attended college and I didn't want to "rat" on him or suggest that ours was anything less than a model family.

I dropped out of school in November, feeling depressed and falling behind under a load of colds, commuting and essays. I was hired at $40 a week by The Telegram, the daily newspaper called the Old Lady of Melinda Street. Editor-emeritus Reginald McEvoy, an octogenarian Weston Collegiate alumnus, had been moved down the street, along with the editorial writers, library and librarian. They needed a secretary and receptionist and I knew how to type and could learn shorthand. This stress-free job, and the daily trips in and out of the city on the Greyhound bus, helped settle my agitation. I "read ahead" and, by fall, was eager to go back to school. My parents borrowed money so I could live in residence until I got my degree.

Outwardly, I had savoir faire but, inwardly, I was brooding over friends' comments that I was "vague," "addicted to the clock" and "falsely modest." I was fatigued, tortured by self recriminations and ego-crippled by a sign I had read long ago in a church basement: "Christ First, Others Next, Self Last". Then, one day, I had a sudden revelation. It occurred to me that the little machine inside my head might be put to work to pull me out of my troubles. I resolved to be my own best friend. I was the same person as the well-meaning one who had bumbled yesterday so I shouldn't be so hard on her. I would support myself and be one healthy ego. This must be what the Bible meant by *Get thee behind me Satan*. After that, whenever I started criticizing and flailing myself, I stopped in my tracks. I began to feel a smug satisfaction with every little victory. Shakespeare's character, Polonius, said to his son, Laertes, "This above all, to thine own self be true." Since infancy, I had lived with the motto of Victoria College, *The truth shall make you free,* and now it had a very personal meaning for me. I wanted to be free but the thing that was keeping me in bonds had to do with religion.

Tanis had graduated in Political Science and Economics and taken a job at Canada Life Assurance Company. In 1953 she married her childhood sweetheart, James Mathers, a mathematics teacher and son of our parents' best friends. In her final year, she had decided to take the leap of faith into Christian beliefs and Jim, too, decided to be a church person. Enid attended Teachers' College and, after getting two years of practical experience, studied at Vic for a year to qualify for a Grade A certificate. In 1954 she married Lorne Creighton, a football and track star from Weston Collegiate who was studying theology at Emmanuel College. These marriages indicated that my sisters would continue to follow the pattern entrenched at the core of our family's life.

I wondered what was going to happen to me and realized I was positioned to inherit the role of black sheep. All the proofs of God (ontological, cosmological, teleological and moral) I had learned in philosophy class had left me cold. Secretly alienated as I felt from the church and my parents, I didn't want to be bad. I didn't want to let anyone have the satisfaction of seeing a "perfect example" fall flat on her face, just because some psychology textbook said it was inevitable. I tried out other churches and causes but they failed to light any sparks.

I was a bridesmaid at a wedding that summer and an usher sought to give me hands-on experience of male anatomy on the lawn of Casa Loma and in the car on the way home. As a compliant, depressed person I felt very vulnerable. The attitude towards sex in our house had been in no way repressive. It just wasn't supposed to exist outside of marriage although, in Cochrane, I had learned that it did. I decided to speak to Father, since this boy who was giving me trouble was the son of an acquaintance of his. He was always closed off in his study and I wanted to jolt him into reality. When I told Father what had happened, he looked at me with great consternation and said, "Did he ejaculate? Did he enter you?" When I said "No" he said "Thanks be to God. Let us pray." Although I appreciated that he didn't get angry and was compassionate, I resented the fact that we couldn't have a one-on-one relationship. God was always in the middle and I was on my own. I think I touched on his ego in this emergency and it was a frightened one. He was afraid that he would fail through me.

In my senior year, I was elected president of Annesley Hall, the girls' residence a.k.a. the Bastion of Virginity. This home to sixty Vic co-eds was named after John Wesley's mother, Susanna Annesley, who set the Methodist pattern for raising children. She considered obedience the basis for all other virtues, since children must learn from their parents until old enough to form their own judgments. They must clean up their plates, speak softly to the servants and be honest, knowing that forgiveness was at hand. She taught her eight children the alphabet on their fifth birthdays, although two of the girls took one-and-one-half days to master it. They learned to pray and read the Bible, and each evening she spent an hour with one child alone. She paid particular attention to John, God's special child who had been saved from a fire in the rectory at the age of six. He grew up to be called "the most influential Englishman since Shakespeare."

I was in a better mood now that I was a senior and could think of two times when I had been a real leader, not just an example. One was when I was a waitress at a summer resort on Sparrow Lake. I took orders from guests seated in the dining hall and then ran through the swinging doors to the kitchen and called them out to the staff behind the steam table. One day I ran in, picked up my tray and found the line stalled. The cook was refusing to serve the waitress ahead of me because she had been twisting a strand of hair around her finger, as if to say "You're nuts." It was just a nervous habit she had. The cook offered to serve me but a big voice from inside me boomed out, "If you don't give her her orders I won't take mine." Then every other waitress behind me said "And neither will I!" "And neither will I!" The boss came over immediately and got things moving.

The other time was when Prof. M. St. A. Woodside invited our Greek and Roman History tutorial to his home in Toronto. We drank tea and chatted but the conversation got thinner and thinner as the sun sank lower and lower and disappeared. The students were waiting for the professor to dismiss his class while the host was waiting for his guests to suggest that they leave. Finally I could stand the tension no longer and murmured, "I think it is time for us to go." All of my classmates jumped up as if they were India-rubber balls that had been waiting to be bounced.

One day I was climbing the narrow staircase leading from the Varsity (the campus newspaper) just as another staffer, a mechanical engineering student, was descending. Our gaze met and I had the sensation of being torpedoed right through his eyes and into his soul. We went out on a foursome the night of Hurricane Hazel and, six days later, he offered me his honor-award pin. I accepted it but kept it on a powder puff inside the music box the Simpsons rep had given me. We dated for three weeks while I checked out his campus reputation, met his family and made my decision. He more than fulfilled the dreams I had had as a seven-year-old but what about the pattern? He had been born and educated in the Calvinist (Presbyterian) tradition. He did not drink except for the occasional liqueur or glass of wine with a meal. I could put him into a biblical perspective as a "son of Martha," the doer, whereas I was a "Mary," the listener. His mother (unfortunately, his father was dead) was a wonderful person and he was very caring towards her. It was a go! Thomas Virany was no longer engaged to a powder puff.

His home was compassionate and moral but not so openly hung up on a huge sense of debt to "the Book" as ours was. His family revolved directly around familial love, culture, education, ambition and good taste. They used the words "excellent," "elegant," "beautiful" and weren't puritanical. Such exuberance made me feel I was casting off shackles and emerging freely into a broader world.

I brought Tom to one of Professor Northrop Frye's lectures to our class of thirteen and sat in the front row with my diamond solitaire flashing. "Nory" and several of his classmates had also met the person they married when they were at Vic. Most students, like myself, did not communicate face to face with Frye because of mutual shyness. Now forty-five, he was world famous for his literary "grammar," Anatomy of Criticism. The two or three times our eyes met in class, I felt we liked each other. I identified with him as the youngest child brought up in a Methodist household saturated with literature and the Bible. I also identified him with Father, since both had studied English, Philosophy & History at Vic and gone on to Emmanuel College. Both had logical, critical, inquiring minds which co-existed with an irrational belief in God.

Frye had got his theology degree on the understanding that he would be a teacher rather than a preacher. When a girl in class asked a question based on Christian assumptions, rather than being an honest query, he rejected it. That is not what we were there for. Yet one of the most endearing things he said to us, as students of English literature, was "We are emotionals not intellectuals." Literature had been empowering individuals to sort through their personal complexes and maladjustments long before psychology was dreamt of. One day, in a lecture on Milton's Paradise Lost, Frye drew a diagram on the blackboard with "fallen man" and "angels" on it. I asked him where "unfallen man" fitted in and he said that was a very searching question. That was the way he taught. He did not give a direct answer because that would close the matter; he wanted me to keep on thinking. He and his wife, Helen, invited our class to their modest home one Sunday for tea and treated us like celebrities. They had no children of their own.

Ever since "Jessie Mac" had told me the source of a depression often lies within a person's family, I had been mulling things over. I felt I had to choose between growing up and being a Christian. I wanted my parents to go on loving me but would they if I gave up the Church? The scriptures are full of pressure to commit yourself to the Lord and encourage others to do the same. When I mentioned this to Tom, he said, "If you put Christ before me and our future children then we shouldn't be getting married." I chose him because in that way I was choosing myself.

We graduated in June, 1955, and were married by Father that September in Durham, Grey County, where he had been called in 1954. Our best man was John Rowe, the chaplain of Hart House, who had been part of our Hurricane Hazel foursome. It looked very good that the groom's closest friend wore a clerical collar. I did not want to upset the all-important pattern, even though marriage and a change of name released me from my ministerial-daughter duties. I no longer had to set an example helpful to my father. As it turned out, the Durham gossips had their day. Some of them did not know how many daughters my parents had but otherwise they were good at counting. When Tanis had a baby on Feb. 4, 1956, they had it all figured out. And to think that I had the nerve to stand up in church in a white dress! Poor Mr. and Mrs. Kell!

Tom and I moved to Montreal and my thoughts turned to starting a career. My parents and their way of life were far away and I was sure we could do better than they had. But English-speaking Montreal was not that big and I had to go crawling to Father's old buddy, Ernie Taylor, for help in finding a job. He was secretary of the international branch of the Montreal YMCA and a "genius of friendship," like Grandfather Ward had been. Soon I was publicity secretary of the Metropolitan Montreal YMCA and Sir George Williams College, which opened that year in the YMCA building and later evolved into Concordia University. It was an exciting job, especially since I handled all the media contacts. I doubled my output by phoning my engineer husband at Northern Electric and soaking up the know-how he had acquired as editor-elect of the Varsity and campus stringer for the Globe & Mail.

I wore my hair short, stopped sleeping with it in rags and pin curls, and ate out every night. I was too busy drinking cappuccino, improving my driving and learning how to ski downhill to go to church that winter. This idyllic sojourn lasted until we both lost our jobs the same week, Tom for being too independent and I for being a woman. It seemed that Ernie had only been able to talk the YMCA brass into giving me my job "until we can find our man." We retreated to Toronto.

I didn't keep close track of my parents but short visits home verified that the battle of the sexes was ongoing and I still cried in church. Mother chafed when she was not in control or getting attention. Father rejected her sensible, obvious advice if he thought he was being bossed too much. I thought their arguments and alliterations, such as Baby Band, Leaders' Lab, Couples' Club and Afternoon Auxiliary, were infantile. Their bland diet, sterile pictures and predictable reading material were a bore. Only The United Church Observer lay on the coffee table.

I had no idea what doggedness it took for Father to get the congregation in Durham (and, later, Flesherton) to agree to add a kitchen and bathroom to their church and pay for it. Nor did I notice that Mother planned beautiful worship services for her women's groups and gave talks on behalf of the native people. My sister Enid, on the other hand, saw how their efforts were apreciated and would be remembered. Lorne was the United Church minister in nearby Priceville and Mother had Enid's help in running an annual vacation school. She felt lucky to be physically close to the parents she had always been emotionally close to. Their tender, loving care had saved her life when she had polio. In the summers, Mother and Father took vive-la-compagnie-type jobs at church camps or attended a school for rural clergymen and their wives.

On a holiday in 1957, Father suffered from jaundice and abdominal pains and X-rays taken after he got home showed several large gall stones. The operation to remove them left him so weak he needed a blood transfusion. Six weeks later, he had to be re-admitted to hospital and operated on again to remove another big stone. He lost forty pounds and looked gaunt for a long while afterwards.

Mother started teaching leathercraft at night school in Flesherton, her first activity outside of the church and her family. She gained a little weight and looked happier. With the arrival of grandchildren my parents baby-sat and hosted ever-larger family gatherings, often including Aunt Clara's and Aunt Mabel's households.

After years of service, Father was elected president of the Toronto Conference of the United Church of Canada which extends from Lake Ontario up to James Bay. During an official tour through the northern part of the territory in 1959, my parents stayed at the home of the Powassan minister. His wife entertained them with after-dinner stories, including the one about an unnamed minister's wife who had left behind the farewell gift which the ladies of the Nakina WA had given her. "I guess I have become a legend," Mother said ruefully, and set her straight on the details.

After we moved back to Toronto, Tom worked at Canadian Press and Maclean-Hunter and I for the YMCA. My job was to get publicity without having a budget and that was right up my alley. Society was so keen to pass on to the baby-boomers the values defended in World War II, that I was able to get ample coverage in the newspapers, radio and TV. I fought and won a feminist battle to get my own office; up until then all females sat in an outer, general area and all men in cubby-holes.

Tom and I lived like bohemians and went in our Volkswagen beetle to see the art museums of New York, Washington, Boston, Chicago, Philadelphia and Baltimore. My cultured Hungarian mother-in-law, Clara Virany, taught me how to cook the very finest dishes. We abandoned the VW for two Citroëns (first an ID costing $3100 and then a DS costing our old car plus $600) and we flew to Europe for three weeks. Upon our return, I discovered I was pregnant. I knew nothing about raising children but my boss at the YMCA said, "All you have to do is love them" and I was sure I could do that.

The religious editor of The Toronto Star gave me a compliment about my father when he found out I was Jack Kell's daughter. "I like him," he said. "He's very earthy." Over lunch in a restaurant with Mother after I had had my baby and was working part-time on a CBC-TV conference on The Real

World of Woman, I told her about a problem I was having. Dr. Camille Laurin, a psychiatrist and later a Québec cabinet minister, was one of the speakers and the advance copy he had submitted of his speech mentioned the sexual organs of the female monkey and female human being explicitly. "Well," said Mother, "they're just as much a part of your body as your nose." I was impressed; she was very earthy too.

Three more grandsons arrived in time to celebrate my parents' thirty-fifth wedding anniversary at their home in Flesherton, Ontario, a rural town of six hundred which was attracting the younger generation of hippies. Mother and Father fit in just fine, I think because of his cut-offs and her unassuming friendliness. Although she was often petty and retiring, she could get along anywhere she had a cleaning woman, a hairdresser and historical novels. The latter kept her mind from whipping itself up into enervating spirals.

In 1963 Mother fell ill and the doctors detected a "menagerie" (as she put it) of coxsackievirus, Asian 'flu, and polio running around in her system. Her arms and face reddened and swelled up grotesquely and she had severe chest pains and belching. After being treated for ten days in hospital, she came home but was told to go back for regular chest x-rays. One of these revealed a spot on her lung: tuberculosis. She knew she carried the antibodies because she had been exposed to this disease when she lived up north. Under the stress of the other illnesses, it had become active instead of latent. She was sent to the Freeport Sanitarium where the spot disappeared but she was kept for two months.

I had never noticed that Father was subject to high and low moods, until he was left alone and seemed vulnerable. Mother's nagging presence relieved him of the compulsion to scold himself. Her type of attention exasperated onlookers but kept him evenly cheerful. It was the flip side of flirtatiousness, playfulness and exhibitionism but at least it was exclusively for him. He sorely missed her. Since their Lemonville days, he had obeyed her order to be home for a cup of tea and petit beurre at 10 a.m., 4 p.m. and 10 p.m.

On his own in the kitchen, Father was quick and competent, frying bacon, eggs, potatoes and "bubble and squeak" (cabbage added to the potatoes) in the cast-iron skillet. He rinsed his china tea cup out right away so it wouldn't stain. My parents always drank milk with their meals; it and the lunch staples of pickled beets, cheddar cheese and canned sardines were always on hand. I was uncomfortable being alone with him. I was afraid that, if I challenged him with some of the scientific agnosticism I had picked up, his whole raison d'être might topple like a stack of cards. He enjoyed having a good argument but I did not. Seeing my parents become ill and weak had made me feel anxious and compassionate. They couldn't die while things between us were unresolved and I was angry.

By 1966, my parents had three more grandchildren and, when Victoria University awarded Father an honorary Doctor of Divinity, I invited everyone to our home after the ceremony. Privately I thought he was making too big a fuss and being egotistical. In those days, I was mostly staying home to practise the arts of love and language-instilling with my newborn daughter and four-year-old son. Tom was a CBC-TV reporter and entertained the country by doing some interviews in the buff at a nudist camp. A contract he later had with Toronto File was not renewed, due to budget cuts, so he switched to teaching.

One day as I sat and sewed, W. Greig Macdiarmid, former general secretary of the YMCA, asked me to phone his wife, Fen. She was beautiful and quite a bit younger than he was. She poached a salmon in her dishwasher for a garden party we attended at their home and she fielded phone calls from me when I was trying to get permission to release a story. The only thing was that when I got this message from Mr. Macdiarmid he had been dead for some time. I paced up and down the room, looking over my shoulder to try to assess what had happened. It was like a dream only I was fully awake. This sort of thing was in our family. Father had received a message from Grandma that she needed him in the middle of one night in 1936. He woke us and bundled us off to Cookstown without knowing until we got there that Uncle Clifton had died. Grandma, who had no phone, was standing at the window expecting Father. Then, in 1940, Uncle Joe came to say good-bye to Aunt Enid the night his ship went down in the Japan Sea. When Mother heard such reports, she just said "I wonder." Father never tried to explain them.

I couldn't imagine that Mrs. Macdiarmid needed me so I summoned up all my resources to dismiss the incident from my mind. However, years later, I found out that Fen had died alone and painfully from cancer, estranged from her only daughter. Father always asked God to forgive us our "sins of omission" and I regard this as one. I could have made a friendly phone call on an impulse without compromising my self-image as a rational person.

I had two meaningful exchanges with Father during this decade. Many of my peers got a financial boost from their parents and, while I knew mine had to save up for a house, I thought I would test the waters. I went into his study and hinted to his back that a little money might come in handy. He swiveled slowly in his desk chair in my direction and said in an emphatic, incredulous tone, "I gave you your life." I retreated meekly but I wanted to yell "Bravo! Spoken like a true man of God, not of Caesar!" My parents did not seem whole to me but at least the reason was not hypocrisy. I admired his toughness and integrity but it is horrible to be made feel like an ingrate. The other exchange took place on the day he got his DD and I asked if he would like to christen our children. He said "No," I should wait until we got settled in a community and then ask our own minister to do it. He was right and my motives weren't. To be honest, I was offering him a sop in an attempt to retain his affection. That year they bought a white frame bungalow in Owen Sound for $11,000 cash and retired.

I gave birth to a second daughter in 1966 and the next fifteen years saw Tom and me raising our three children from diapers to diplomas. We lived in Ottawa, since he took refuge in a government job as a patent examiner when teaching proved to be unkind. He moonlighted as a TV journalist or translator and I as an editor, free-lance writer, sales rep or office temp.

"Granny" and "Grandpa" were favorites with our kids during their regular visits but I still disliked Mother for reasons I couldn't identify. I was busy trying to make our own marriage and family life happy and not become a nag.

20

Our Parents Retire, Leaving Us To Work Out
Our Own Faiths

My parents had a good time flying off to England four times and Australia once to visit relatives and historical sites. But Father missed the old way of ocean-crossing, where he could exercise his debating talents, critical training and Hebrew scholarship by getting into arguments out on the water. Someone always reacted to the sight of a clerical collar. One young man once asked him if he could turn *water into wine* or get *bread from* a *stone*. When Father said "No" the young man asked, "Well, what can you do?" Father replied, "What Jesus did—go about teaching, helping people and doing good." Another youth once said much of what was written in the Bible was untrue. Father disarmed him by agreeing on some points but adding, "Christianity is much more firmly based than you suppose."

My parents retired and moved to Owen Sound, where Enid taught, in 1966. Father became assistant minister at Westside United Church and also joined the Grey County Historical Society, sang in a Glee Club and filled out tax returns for residents at Lee Manor Retirement Home. He set himself a goal of preaching at every little, old, rural church in the county and succeeded in being invited (mostly on anniversaries) to fifty-two -- a different one for every Sunday of the year. He and Mother were often invited to a home for dinner after the service. His sermons were better than ever, less wooden because he didn't spend so much time preparing them.

Mother continued to teach her weekly night class in Flesherton. Every piece of leather craft she produced, be it purse, wallet, belt, brooch or desk set, was beautifully, expertly carved and often colored. On the domestic side, her chicken casserole was a big hit at the ministerial society's monthly pot-luck suppers. When Father and friends spent a summer adding a back porch and car port to the bungalow, she was always ready with tea and cookies for them and any wives who dropped by. Quite often, Enid came home from school to find Father working in her garden and Mother preparing a pot of tea.

They were usually together, except when Father took off alone in their blue Honda. One Christmas when I was there, I saw how Mother's nerves began to accelerate almost the instant he turned out of the driveway. He was carefree as a henpecked husband on the loose but she was fretful as a soldier's wife with a premonition. She envisioned all sorts of calamities befalling him on the wintry, narrow country roads. 'I hope he doesn't have a flat tire...Maybe he's gotten stuck in the snow...He might have to walk for miles to get help...and catch pneumonia...I told him not to go out without his scarf but he won't listen!...I hope he doesn't try to push the car out by himself and strain his heart...or have a heart attack...He will insist on taking chances!...He should be home soon...It's time to put the kettle on ...unless he's collided with another car at one of those intersections with no stop signs...What's keeping Dad?... Why isn't he home?...It would be just like him to get himself killed and...' By the time she spotted the car at the end of the street by craning her neck from her post at the livingroom window, her nerves were so exhausted she was ready to let loose with a tirade. Mother loved Father deeply but she wasn't nice to him on the surface. Father did not love Mother passionately but he was caring and did, in the long run, pay attention to her. A truce was declared when they had tea and a cookie with their books open and the radio tuned to classical music.

In 1973, Mother and Father took Tanis and Enid on a trip to show them their birthplaces. They visited Dulas McIvor in Winnipeg (Alice was now dead) and Esther Gaudin, who was now Esther Ross, in Transcona. She had sent Father a copy of her wedding picture in 1935 but he hadn't seen her since 1929. When he did, he found himself still in love. So was she—but not with him. Of course, none of these personal things were spoken about. Father was perturbed to see that Esther didn't have nice things and no man appeared to be sharing the house with her. She said nothing about her husband but her three grown children were doing well.

In Norway House, my family stayed at the home of the Very Rev. Stan McKay. He grew up on the Fisher Lake Reserve and became the first native person to be elected moderator of the United Church of Canada. One of his first reforms was to hold a training session for Indian elders to qualify them for full time jobs in the church. Father was no doubt trying to assess his record on the mission field during this visit. McKay's views were as follows, but the ratings are mine:

(1) The missionaries should speak Cree and encourage the people to develop their own leaders (B+ for Father) (2) The missionaries should be specially trained for this service, since it takes a person two years to get accustomed to the life (A for Father) (3) It is not good enough to have local elders serve as interpreters for white pastors (B for Father) (4) The native elders should be licensed to administer the sacraments and perform marriages (C for the Church) (5) The Indians are a deeply spiritual people; white men could learn much from them if they listened (A for Father.) This visit took place before revelations of sexual abuse in the residential schools had surfaced (A for Father's good behavior.)

At this writing, the scenery at Oxford House is as beautiful as ever, tuberculosis has virtually disappeared, the population has more than tripled and the people live in frame houses. The United Church has created a self-governing All Native Circle

Conference to replace "mission fields" and has apologized for "seeking to impose our civilization as a condition of accepting the gospel." The Catholics and Protestants now co-operate closely. (Father would be happy with all these improvements.)

But the people are still overcrowded and many walk around on dialysis because the amount of carbohydrates found in the white man's agricultural foods can cause diabetes or kidney ailments. (In teaching them to grow vegetables, Father had hoped to improve their diet and give them a sense of mastery over nature so they would be less superstitious.) According to John Thompson, the present United Church minister at Oxford House, families are torn apart over whether to re-open the doors once closed on their traditional culture. Highly-financed, fundamentalist preachers from the United States entertain the young with bands, sweep them off their feet and victimize them in a new way. The people find it hard to think for themselves because they've always been controlled. They bring their old and dying back to their United Church "roots" for funerals. (Father would see that there is still much work left to do.)

After my family got back from their trip out west, Enid came to visit us in our home. She had been speaking to Aunt Clara who, on a bus trip to Lachute, Quebec, had sat beside Raymond Cassie, the inspector who had come to our school in Cochrane. As they bumped along, she mentioned us and he told her he remembered Enid and me as being the nicest and smartest girls in Central Public School. (Tanis was in high school at the time so he didn't know her.) In fact, my IQ was the highest he had ever tested. This was the best compliment (ego food) I had got since I was a baby behind crib bars and it made up for the ones I didn't get which I thought were my due. (Was it the adrenalin, I wonder?) I wanted a full-time job and applied to the civil service and other places but didn't get one.

Around this time in London, Ontario, tests determined that Allan, Tanis and Jim's youngest son, had been born with one extra chromosome. He was a beautiful child although severely mentally retarded, epileptic, partially blind and unable to talk or walk. Tanis groomed and dressed him with loving care.

Jim carried him around until they were able to obtain a large, electric, umbrella stroller. Their four older children looked after him tenderly and adoringly. Sadly, Allan died at the age of eight. The family mourned him greatly and Tanis, a high-school teacher now, was in a state of deep shock and sorrow.

That fall we bought a house in Aylmer, Quebec, and moved to the other side of the Ottawa River. We joined Aylmer United Church and attended every second Sunday (Tom less often) but I still couldn't sit through a church service without dissolving into tears. It was the same involuntary emotion that overcame me if I watched an episode of Lassie Come Home on TV. I thought it might have something to do with the resistance I was harboring inside my heart towards Mother. I mentioned this to my minister, Richard DeLorme, and he urged me to have a talk with her.

This sounds like an easy thing to do but, whereas I had had three or four significant conversations with Father during my lifetime, I had never had a single one with Mother. She didn't know who I was. I considered her a big nothing. Ever since she had insulted me at a very young age by saying I was supposed to be red-haired, twin boys I had put up a wall between us. No one knew what I had done; they just thought I was "like that."

On the occasion of Mother's seventy-fifth birthday, we celebrated at an elegant old farmhouse which had been turned into a restaurant. She looked around at her three children, three sons-in-laws and nine grandchildren and said, "Look at all I have accomplished since coming to Canada!" This was a rare moment of self-satisfaction. For once, she wasn't comparing herself unfavorably to women who had careers, were better housekeepers or, like Anna Gaudin, had had books written about them. Mother was surprised to find out it was I who had suggested the party. Usually Father came up with the idea for celebrating birthdays and anniversaries, particularly his own; he had such a sense of history and living out one's book of days. His congregation gave him a desk set that year to commemorate the fiftieth anniversary of his ordination.

Enid's husband was late for the party and later we found out why. He had been cheating on her with a younger woman who had just given birth to his baby daughter. Of course, the whole town knew what was going on but Enid had believed Lorne was out nights doing family counseling. He had left the ministry, become a probation officer, then a high school guidance teacher and a candidate for the NDP. She had a mild heart attack from the shock and was on valium until my parents nursed her back to health. Father was thoroughly disgusted with his son-in-law and, for many years, was hard put to forgive him. When Enid got better, she completed her university degree and became a special education teacher. Ten years later, she married Hugh McDiarmid, a retired newspaper publisher and businessman who was more than twenty years her senior.

Today, Enid, a much treasured Owen Sound widow, continues to cultivate our parents' network of friends and relatives as well as her own. She is a pillar of Knox United Church and a generous supporter of community causes, such as a self-help program for abusive husbands. All the fuss and trauma Tanis and I got into vis à vis Father and our religious beliefs never did make a whole lot of sense to her. In recent years, Lorne apologized for having courted her too hard and pressured her into marrying him. She told him, "Don't dwell on it. Look at it this way. We have two wonderful children." Sixteen years of happiness with Hugh made up for all the heartbreak and embarrassment she had suffered.

After Allan's death, Tanis turned to yoga. At age five she had offered to be like Samuel, who sat in the temple and listened for the voice of God. When she heard the story of the girl who was revived from death, she asked Father if it was true but he said it hadn't really happened. If this was so, she concluded she didn't have to believe a whole lot of other things either. She had read the same church-basement sign which upset me and, as the eldest, she identified with "Christ First." That meant the Christlikeness of being last. Mother told her that she should let the younger ones go first so they wouldn't cry. She grew up deferring to her parents, her sisters (even when we grew taller than she was,) the Church and the kids at school. But she could only go on like that for so long before the real, determined, controlling child came through. It was only when she got married that she decided to be a Christian believer. Practising yoga now led her to realize the spiritual world was more than just the imagination.

Ann Kelly, a reporter for The Owen Sound Sun-Times, wrote a feature about Father's "well seasoned" life in 1976. The accompanying picture showed him in his element, happily pulling up a bunch of carrots from his garden. At this point, I knew next to nothing about what my parents had done before I was born so my eyebrows were raised when I read:

"He was the first man to take a Bible among the Cree Indians at God's Lake...He's done farming, pulled teeth with pliers (on one occasion he even pulled one of his own) treated burns and ax cuts with limited medical supplies, cooked on a wood stove by the light of an Aladdin's lamp,..." As for Mother, I read:

"When Mrs. Kell arrived at the mission station she had short, bobbed hair. The reaction of the school children was to cut their long braids. One by one, that's what they did...A radio, the school teacher and the employees at the Hudson's Bay post were Mrs. Kell's only links with a civilization outside the mission..."

I tried to imagine Mother being a teen-age idol or living a rough life. These days she never even went out to look at Father's vegetable garden. The article continued:

"The birth of their first child, Tanis (Indian for daughter) took place at Norway House, a six-day trip by sled. They made the trek six weeks before the baby was born, sleeping along the trail en route."

All I remembered was Mother mentioning a trip that was "too risky" and carping at Father that, "You should have taken me out before Christmas, not in January."

Two or three times in church Father had shown his slides of Indian mission work. To me it looked like a miserable, unattractive assignment which he did heaven knows why. Was this story suggesting my parents had done what they wanted to do and actually had fun? Nowadays, Mother's church work bolstered her soul but did nothing for her ego. When anyone suggested she was a good Christian, she would say, "Oh no I'm not; not really." At least her eyes lit up when she received a beautiful northern landscape painting by John Landon, an artist of partly native heritage she met when they both taught night school. She hung it over the livingroom fireplace.

In 1978, Jim and Tanis were amazed to see their eldest daughter, Kathy, suddenly change from an angry, third-year engineering student into a peaceful, productive adult. After a few months, she invited her mother and father to her water baptism and urged them to jump in after her. They both agreed to, in their own time. In the next year, Tanis began waking up with hymns playing in her mind and "a chance encounter led to a walk with God" (her words.) She wrote Father a letter about her deeper faith, saying she wasn't criticizing or condemning him, but he didn't reply. He was devastated that the daughter of the winter ecstasy had rejected his brand of practical Christianity. I think his ego was frightened, hurt and dismayed. While still a United Church member, Tanis joined an international interdenominational evangelical organization (AGLOW) and became a leader.

Father, a very grounded person, was never transformed by a sudden, dramatic, religious awakening of the type which John Wesley, the founder of Methodism, underwent. While sailing home in 1778 after leading a rigidly doctrinaire Anglican mission in Georgia, Wesley confessed to two Moravian missionaries on board that he was not a true Christian. They said, "Do you have Jesus in your heart?" and pointed out that it is not enough to serve Jesus as a servant; one must serve him as a son. This is more than a trust with God; it is a oneness. It is the difference between a simile and a metaphor; you can be *like* Christ, or you can *be in* Christ *and have* him *in you*. After a sudden warming of the heart at a bible meeting in England, Wesley was transformed. He became a social reformer and evangelizer of the masses, spreading the message that salvation is possible for every person through faith alone. Such passion led his brother, Charles, to compose Hark, the Herald Angels Sing, Love Divine All Loves Excelling and other immortal hymns.

As Tanis's faith grew through prayer and bible-reading, her family (certainly I) could always depend on her for supportive, sound advice. She hugged bag ladies, helped women cancer patients get better by forgiving those they were angry at, took homeless people into her house, fed the poor and invited the mentally ill up to her summer cottage. She was surely the Mother Tanisa of London, Ontario. After a decades-long struggle against adult leukemia, chronic asthma and the effects of a stroke, she died suddenly of a stroke on July 15, 2002. She felt at peace with Father because she knew he was acting according to his light in following the prophet's words, *What does the Lord require of thee but to do justice, love mercy and walk humbly with your God in his path.*

On a trip home to Owen Sound after my parents had down-sized to an apartment, I waited for my eighty-year-old mother to go into the bedroom and then followed her. Without waiting for her to turn around I said falteringly, "Mom, I don't think we've always had the greatest relationship." She turned around and her perceptive blue eyes were opened the widest I had ever seen them. She just stared at me and blinked twice. Then she said, "I'm so glad you told me" and held out her arms. I didn't even have to mention red-haired twin boys or the wall I had erected between us. We just embraced and cried and understood each other completely. This was *forgiveness*; my burden was gone. From then on I unabashedly loved Mother and enjoyed my parents' presence when they visited us.

In 1981 I became editor and part-owner of our new local newspaper, The Aylmer Bulletin. The deal was that my business partner and his wife would look after the money end, Tom would help me after work with the editorial side, and our house would be the newspaper's address. It became a community hub, somewhat like the parsonage in Thistletown. I was very busy but found that if I read my notes before I went to sleep my stories almost wrote themselves next morning.

By now, I was beginning to focus on the end of my life, rather than the middle, but I was still confused about my beliefs and philosophy. Before I was ready to proclaim anything, I wanted to check out a few things. For example, Why do we need to have religion in the first place? and, if it is so important, Why do we have to put our heads inside a shell in order to have it? For answers, I turned to the books of my old professor, Northrop

Frye. Through his Fearful Symmetry I had already encountered William Blake's maxims, All Religions Are One, Exuberance is Beauty and There Is No Natural Religion. When Frye's two studies of the Bible and literature came out in the early eighties, I gave The Great Code to Father for his birthday and asked Tom to give me Words with Power for mine. As a Victoria College punster once put it, "The truth shall make you Frye." It wasn't easy reading but I knew I was in the presence of a great mind who wanted to help me clear up my thinking on these subjects.

I didn't know how devastating it is to have a close member of one's family suffer a nervous breakdown until I myself experienced it. Professional advice and care helped a lot but I also needed to talk to my roses and spend much time in prayer. The phrase, *Give us this day our daily bread*, meaning to live one day at a time and leave oneself open to receiving spiritual as well as physical support, helped me cope.

Conclusion

Celebrating My Parents' Lives In

a Spirit of Ego-Redemption

Ordination Anniversary, 1976

21

Dying Well In Love's Embrace, As Methodists Are Wont To Do

ather's favorite text was *The Word was made flesh and dwelt among us*. In his ministry, he strove to get people to look at how Jesus behaved when he was on earth and to follow his example. Father believed simple, honest, devout people were at the heart of the power of the Church. Preaching clichés and emphasizing enigmatic features of Christ's divinity drove them away and caused the Church to lose credibility. He feared ministers weren't preaching what they were learning in theological college in this day and age—namely, that the miracles were embroidery, added on to the first accounts of Jesus's life in order to attract converts. He believed it was the simple people's faith that allowed Jesus to heal them. Because five hundred Gallileans alive at the time testified they saw the resurrected Christ, the Easter message is real. It proclaims that good will triumph over evil and life over death.

In 1981 Father wrote a lengthy essay on The Life of Jesus of Nazareth which he hoped might become the basis for a compulsory course of study for prospective ministers. One of his conclusions was, "We should get rid of such weird notions as that Jesus was born without a human father, that he could do all sorts of magical tricks and that his physical body could ascend into the sky and will come back again sometime." He sent copies to two hundred Church leaders and heads of theological colleges and got forty replies. Former moderator Angus

MacQueen wrote, "Your emphasis on Jesus the Man is a very necessary one. Stressing that the word was made flesh (in other words, that God was in Christ) is a very different thing from saying that Jesus was God, period. That's a clear heresy and yet I am appalled at the "Jesusolatry" being preached today." Former moderator George Tuttle wrote, "You are obviously opposed to reducing Jesus to a mysterious figure theologically but I fear you offer another reduction in confining yourself to the historical figure." Father didn't manage to set up a course but he did get a lot of historicity out of his system.

He also wrote a paper on the virgin birth, saying he rejected the doctrine for a number of reasons: (1) The word for a young maiden had been translated as "virgin" (2) None of the disciples recorded this story and (3) It was Joseph's lineage that made Jesus a descendant of King David. Father did not need a supernatural myth to make him believe profoundly that Jesus was "100% divine and 100% human."

My parents traveled out west by train and rental car one last time to visit cousins and friends and Esther again invited them to dinner. Her son had recently arranged for her divorce from the man she had married in 1935 but she kept that a secret. What had really happened was that he went overseas with the RCAF in 1940, after they had had three children, and, once there, fell in love with a Scottish woman. They climbed the social ladder and drank away all his money, while he continued to write devoted letters to Esther. At the end of the war, she found out he didn't intend to return and she and her children were left desperately poor. Angry as she was, she carried a torch for him over the years and would have taken him back in a moment had he come. Being a loyal knight, Father still loved Esther although he did not know her tragic story. He could just see that she was not as happy and wealthy as he would have wished.

My parents, avid subscribers to The Aylmer Bulletin, visited us spring and fall with Father bringing along his overalls and rubber boots so he could work in the garden. I sometimes caught him pausing to lean on his shovel to smile up at the geese flying over. But the mortal bodies were beginning to give out on the impeccable souls.

In the winter of '82-'83, Father frightened us all by "taking a turn" (his phrase for having a mild heart attack) while shoveling snow. He also suffered from a persistent, dull ache in the heart and low blood pressure. Mother's blood pressure was high and she suffered from angina. That March they both passed out at the same time, with Mother breaking her ankle as she fell. The neighbor from across the hall came to their rescue, they were admitted to hospital and Enid dashed over from her school. A few months later, Mother got a stroke warning but then both of them rallied. That summer, Enid brought them to Aylmer and Father took the helm of our sailboat out on Lake Deschênes. In 1986, they moved into a seniors' lodge where they could prepare their own meals and drive a car but be under the same roof as all the amenities: Keen-Age Klub, convenience store, chapel, hairdresser, dining room, hospital and morgue. They could press a buzzer to summon help if needed.

Forty of us gathered outdoors at Tanis and Jim's cottage on Father's ninetieth birthday as he distributed a bag of coins from his collection to each grandchild. He led us in prayer and made a speech ending with, "and I certainly married the right woman." Mother smiled sweetly but I thought he could have complimented her a little more warmly than that. She insisted on having another celebration in November to mark their sixtieth wedding anniversary. Ellen Hay of The Owen Sound Sun Times wrote an article, printed with a picture of them inclining their heads together, and I particularly liked these excerpts:

"Mrs. Kell: We often disagree—I think there is an obstinate streak in both of us—but I think we really do love each other. And we have had an extremely interesting life."

"Dr. Kell: My philosophy for a good marriage comes from the actress Ellen Terry: "I forgive everybody before I go to bed." I decided early on not to make money too important a part of my life."

"Dr. and Mrs. Kell: "We are especially proud of our daughters. They've been a great treasure to us."

Father sometimes tried to put Mother in a good mood by putting his arm around her and holding her hand when they sat on the chesterfield. She was not such a sentimental person. Cousin Mary recalls that, on one visit, Mother sat down on the sofa, patted the seat and said "Come, Jack. We haven't said our prayer together yet today." Father wanted her to remember the adventures they had when they were first married but she never wrote anything down until he nudged her to do so. When her turn came to tell her life story at the Koffee Klatsche, her voice was too croaky to be understood. Her body was also getting weak and she declared "This is the end!" when her ailing legs tripped and she fell. Not great in emergencies except with horses, poor Father said "Get up, Old Girl!" and she did, with his and Enid's help.

His health problems also mounted. A main artery from his heart was disintegrating and nothing could be done to fix it. He asked the doctor how long he had left to live and the doctor said "Two or three years." Father recorded these bald facts in his diary while Mother, seemingly left in the dark, wrote in hers that his blood pressure was good.

By now, Uncle Eric, Aunt Doris, Aunt Enid, Aunt Mabel, Uncle Frank and Cousin Albert were all gone. Aunt Clara and Father wrote a little booklet called A Tribute to Our Parents, describing how they had been brought up in a Methodist household by parents who were honest, generous, neighborly and broadminded. There were a few Anglicans and Presbyterians in Cookstown, and the rare Baptist or Pentecostal, but nothing as exotic as a Catholic or Jew. Shortly after the booklet was published, Aunt Clara died and Father sank into a depression.

Mother and Father moved upstairs into a one-room apartment with no kitchen, dispersed their furniture and belongings and sold their car. His alternating high and low moods had always been tied to the weather and here the atmosphere was oppressive. A friend drove him around to photograph all the vanishing little country churches in the county. His granddaughter, Anne, who bought his car, drove him down to Victoria College to walk in an academic procession. He tried to keep up his interest in other topics and wrote letters to his old girlfriends, Suzy and Esther.

Irene Bracher, Mother's high-school friend and the sister of her long-lost-love, Victor, came over from England for a visit and Tanis and Jim invited them all up to the cottage. Now came news that Uncle Roy had passed away and, on the way to Barrie for the funeral, Father sat alone in the middle of the back seat without a safety belt, stiff, silent and fighting back tears. Suddenly he blurted out, "I married the wrong woman. I should have married Esther." Normally Father's ego didn't erupt; he only revealed it in his conversations with God, and occasionally with Mother. But here it was. He had never stopped fantasizing about what might have been and wondering whether he should have waited for Esther.

He knew from the last time he saw her that she had not had a good life and it was all his fault. If only he had listened to his heart sixty-five years ago and been brave enough to admit to his boss that he was in love with his fifteen-year-old daughter! He had chosen the wrong path and had ended up in this hell of his own making. He had pressured Mother into loving him and that was the only reason she had sacrificed everything to come to Canada and be his wife. He could have spared her this life which had been too stressful for her. Tanis and Jim reassured Father that he had not made any such grave errors. Then he said, "I don't think I should tell this to Mom." She was his best friend and he always told her everything, as long as it wouldn't hurt her.

Back home in their cramped little room, Mother sat in her chair and Father balked at being kept under her thumb. They got on each other's nerves and he missed his car. With his body language he was saying he wanted to get out. She picked this up on her antenna and reacted with the venomous jealousy of a woman who knows she has a rival. She didn't let him have one of the chocolates Rene had given her, even when he pleaded for it. When Enid took him out to the shopping mall, he trailed along behind her bent over double, shuffling his feet. He worried about whether he had enough money to take care of Mother but Jim and Enid offered to help out.

Then the weather improved. Father remembered he was

an example and cheered up. All his life he had had some project or other, such as finding out how artist Tom Thomson died, or tearing down old churches to replace them with seniors' apartments. Now he had a new project—his funeral. He would use it as an occasion to rally his clan, the descendants of his forty-four first cousins from across the land. They would all gather in Cookstown United Church to celebrate their Methodist heritage!

I had planned to take time off in August to see my parents but when I phoned in July Father said "Come now." As I drove them up to the cottage he sat beside me looking vulnerable and Mother sat behind us sounding agitated. He told me she imagined things and it was very sad to see such a wonderful intellect deteriorate. When we got there, Mother said almost exactly the same thing about him. He was obsessed with planning his own funeral and was fantasizing that his far-off relatives would want to come. He had sent the funeral director in Flesherton instructions to conduct the service in Cookstown, along with a check to cover the expense of transporting "the remains." The funeral director had returned the letter and check to Mother, who wanted to handle the arrangements at home rather than impose on the Cookstown people.

Thinking of Father as a person who had always shown professional detachment towards death, I told him he should leave the planning of his funeral to others. After all, he wouldn't be there and its purpose was to help the family cope with their grief. We all loved him and were going to miss him very much. As soon as I said it, I realized from the look in his eye how cruel I had been and felt sorry. However, he didn't hold it against me. When it was time for me to go he insisted on carrying my briefcase up the hill to the car, although he was very frail. He handed it over to me ceremoniously because he wanted to help me with my writing. That was the last time I saw him.

On Aug. 8, 1988, Enid phoned to say that Father had passed away. She had eaten dinner with Mother and Father and ridden the elevator with them back up to their room. He had gone into the bathroom and emerged clutching his stomach and saying,

"I am a very sick man." "Dying" was not in his vocabulary. Then he collapsed and Mother leaned forward in her chair, pulled him up towards her and hugged him in her arms. Great actress that she was, in that final moment she was not only herself but also the beautiful fifteen-year-old Esther loving him and his embittered, eighty-four-year-old mother telling him he had done the right thing. For sixty-one years, Mother had been so dedicated to helping Father she almost forgot that what she wanted most was to make him happy. As if she had asked him to *Lift up the light of thy countenance upon us and grant us peace,* he looked at her with a beautiful smile illuminating his face. The death rattle in his throat was the only way he had left to applaud their wonderful life together. As John Wesley once said when cornered in a debate, "Whatever else you may say about us Methodists, we die well."

Mother was very sad to feel Father body's fall limp in her arms and shook her head, saying "And I didn't let him have one of my chocolates." At least she was happy she had committed him into God's hands with a smile on his face, knowing he had been a good and faithful servant. She too had completed her job as his helpmate in their practical Christian ministry. The epitaph she gave him when she lifted her head was to say that he was "almost great." I'm sorry she couldn't have said he was "really great," or that they couldn't have told each other that they were "great" at any point in their marriage. They considered self-congratulation un-Christian but I think it would have made them happier.

Cookstown United Church was undergoing renovations so the funeral had to (surely Father would understand) take place in Owen Sound. The Rev. Douglas Kaufman said he imagined Father was with us in his habitual pew as the crowd of hundreds sang his favorite hymns, Praise, My Soul, the King of Heaven and Come, Let Us Sing of a Wonderful Love. While not an egotistical man, he was gregarious and glad to be noticed as he heartily belted out a hymn.

As news of Father's passing spread, Mother and Tanis received letters of condolence from Esther. She said she was grateful God had called him away now, rather than letting him see what was happening (referring to the debate over homosexual clergy and the accusations of sexual abuse in the Indian residential schools.) She never mailed an angry letter-to-the-editor she wrote canceling her church membership because she died first of a sudden heart attack. Her family and friends held her funeral in the church, and the house her parents had provided when she was destitute went to her children.

In her loneliness after Father's death, Mother became confused and started hallucinating. At times she was paranoid or else wandered up and down the hall, "looking for Jack." She suffered two or three minor strokes and then a major one. She lost control over some of her muscles, was confined to a wheelchair and had to be transferred to the hospital. The doctor forewarned us that a patient's personality sometimes changes as a result of a stroke, making it difficult for the family. A change did occur but it wasn't at all hard to take. She became the most peaceful, happiest, most-visited person in the ward and flirted with Tom when we came to see her. At the mention of the words "tennis" or "Jack" her eyes gleamed and her face creased in a broad, toothy smile. Enid fed her dinner every night, right up until she died in her sleep on September 13, 1990. At her funeral, we played the Lord's Prayer, since it was the only tape selection in the funeral parlor which she would have considered "good" music. Even Lorne wanted to help carry her coffin out to the hearse but so many other men had already offered he was not needed.

22

Savoring a Little Bit of Earthy Swank

When the estate of the man who didn't want to make money too important was liquidated, each of his heirs received a tidy sum. He had invested his retirement earnings in bonds at a time when interest rates were at a record high. The family donated a memorial pulpit chair to the chapel of Lee Manor in his honor. His sermons and papers were left neatly filed and a flight bag bulged with his pocket diaries. Mother's papers were locked in a metal box and some old albums and mementos lay in a cardboard carton. The only advice she left was a penciled note saying, "I have found in my life that it is easy to figure out what one's faults are but not so easy to know what to do about them." Father's copy of The Great Code was bequeathed to me, leaving me in the hands of the United Church guru he had walked with in an academic procession.

He had scribbled in the margins of the first ten pages but then either stopped reading or gave up being a rival. In 1991, when Frye died, I bought a copy of The Double Vision in which he tells theology grads what he really believes. As a literary critic, he emphasizes the "word" (not the "flesh," as Father had) and says the Bible must be read as it was written—in the language of myth and metaphor. The Bible doesn't care about history. If Father had had a debate with Frye, I think Father would have lost. He'd have had to acknowledge that the spiritual vision (myth and metaphor) of the Bible, not the natural vision (history) of it, gives faith its energy. Both were very forthright men. For my part, I must agree with Frye since what I loved most about Father's preaching was the way he took a text and illuminated it on many levels. I think Father had a lot of *Christ in him* but he probably would have said "Oh, pshaw" if I'd told him so. Although he was a minister, he kept his relationship with God completely private.

One day in 1993, when I was still beset by grief and anxiety over a dear one's illness, six notes of music crept into my head. I knew they were the beginning of a hymn which I had learned long ago, when I was a little example swinging my legs in a pew at Fairbank United Church. The frustrating thing was that I could not remember the title of the hymn nor any of its words. I could have sloughed off the notes as being of no importance but I had done that once before, when Mr. Macdiarmid called me. This time I followed the lead.

I found my dog-eared hymnbook with the musical scores in it and sat down, turning it over page by page from the beginning. So many hymns I hadn't thought about since I was a little girl. It was a slow process, reading the first six notes of every hymn and seeing if they jibed with the ones playing over and over again inside my head. At last it was there in front of me, no. 403, How Firm a Foundation. I read it through, all five verses, slurping them in like nourishment for the thirsty soul. Every word was bang on my present situation. Whoever wrote it had known what I was going through and what help I needed. All the superlatives about God were true because I could imagine them and was validating them by my need for support and my willingness to believe. As I sat at the piano, pounding the keys, the notes were just as good at communicating as the words. This old hymn stood up to me; its power just seemed to get stronger under my day-after-day abuse. I acted out my sadness and desperation and in return was fed relief and courage. Things began to improve and after three more years our children, our treasures, emerged with sparkling colors. Our numbers have increased and, as I write, we have a daughter-in-law, a son-in-law and five grandchildren. Our family has always meant the world to Tom and me.

I was overwhelmed to think that this hymn, written long

ago and sung by my Kell and Wooller great-grandparents, had come to offer its help when I was in need. It was just *standing at the door and knocking*, waiting for me to open it up. I felt a related sense of homecoming when I went to the Kell reunion, after an absence of some fifty years. I was greeted with "Hello, Margaret" by people I didn't recognize, except for family traits like glasses and leanness. Father, the patriarch of the clan, had attended faithfully over the years and kept everyone informed about the activities of "the girls."

How Firm a Foundation is no. 660 in the new United Church hymnbook and when I called it out at a recent hymn-sing the visiting minister said, "This one we have to stand up for." I remembered the joke we used to make in church about not remaining seated on the all-too-firm foundations of our behinds. I finally realized that, corny as it is in some respects, I could never stray far from my family's faith, even if I wanted to. My place lies here, in this tradition. I attend the 175-year-old Aylmer United Church regularly once a month and I don't even cry. Like Victoria College and my great-grandparents' household, it was founded by Methodist circuit preachers fanning out from Upper Canada.

When I think of my parents now, I picture them in their last embrace. Father is mostly composted into the earth to help fertilize the seeds of truth he sowed but he still grounds Mother's sea of nerves as she absorbs him with her love. He is sad that the vision that illuminated and unified Canada in his time has been betrayed and is at best only a footnote to history. However, his attitude would be that the Church has gone through difficult times before and, in the end, the true spirit of Christ will prevail.

He once referred to this framework he had for living as "a crutch." Maybe Father felt he had "married the wrong woman" in the symbolic sense that he could have had a more consummated religious faith. Mother's personality never drew out of him all the exuberance he wanted to express. If Father did have flaws, I just love him all the more.

The title of this book recalls the ninth-century community

of Irish Catholic monks in Kells, Ireland, who copied and illustrated the Holy Scriptures. They produced The Book of Kells, the earliest, most beautifully illuminated manuscript in western civilization. It would be a stretch for me to claim lineage from them but my family did try to illuminate the gospels by the way they lived their daily lives. Father's death marked the end of the "project of art" of an adventuresome knight and lady who threw in their lots with God and each other. They were of "la compagnie" of heroes and heroines who bore the banner of the United Church of Canada over a young, green and blue land imbued with a vision of itself as a shining example to others. No church in history had had such confidence that it could do the right thing by the individual, the country and the world. Peacemaker Lester Pearson and literary critic Northrop Frye embodied the greatness in this tradition. The names of Kathleen (meaning purity) and John (meaning by the grace of God) are woven into the tapestry of this great Canadian epic.

As the embrace fades into memory, I can still picture my mother's friendly smile and twinkling, port girl's eyes. I think it tickled her ego and warped Ward sense of humor to have backed into becoming a legend in her own time. The gift of crystal from the ladies of the Nakina WA still sparkles in my diningroom, the ermine-tail hat turns heads, the Indian princess's slippers dance and the birchbark sewing basket preserves its raspberry hue. She has escaped from the outer reaches of immortality to go on sharing "a little bit of swank" with me. After all, she didn't have just a life, she had a cariole ride. And, thanks to this labor of redeeming coupons from the stores of memory, she knows I'll give the Misses Greene the book she promised them but never found time to write.

Bibliography

Books

Cree-English Dictionary, Fr. Gérard Beaudet, OMI, Wuerz Publishing Ltd., 1995

A Dictionary of the Cree Language, the Church of England in Canada, 1938

Métis Cree Dictionary, Anne Anderson, 1997

The Halifax Disaster December 6, 1917, Ernest Fraser Robinson, Vanwell Publishing, St. Catharines, 1997

The Scottish Tradition in Canada edited by W. Stanford Reid, 1988

For Bread and a Better Future , Anna Reczynska, 1996

I Have Lived Here Since The World Began , Arthur J. Ray, 1996

The Hymnary, United Church of Canada

The Naval Service of Canada, Vol I, "Its Official History", Gilbert Norman Tucker

The Far Distant Ships, Joseph Schull

RCN in Retrospect, 1910-1968, edited by James A. Boutilier

Knights in Armour, Edward S. Woods

The Blue Guide: England, edited by L. Russell Muirhead, 1950

Pregnancy, Gordon Bourne

A Tribute to Our Parents, Jack and Clara Kell

Year Book and Directory, the United Church of Canada, 1996

Year Book of the United Church of Canada, 1926, 1927, 1928, 1929

Taylor Statten, C.A.M. Edwards

David Copperfield, Charles Dickens

Canada's First Nations, Olive Patricia Dickason

Pioneer Missionary Journals, 1857

Anna and the Indians, Nan Shipley

The Popular History of Methodism, John Telford

The Popular History of John Wesley, John Telford

The Story of a Hundred Years, 1845-1945, Wesley Church, Portsmouth

Gospel Hymns compiled by P.P. Bliss and Ira D. Sankey, Copp Clark 1881

The Call of the Wild, Jack London

Canada, an Outline History, J.A. Lower

The Legends of Wesakecha, Anne Anderson

The Stories of the Swampy Cree, Charles Clay

Canada, Land of Many Dreams, Robyn Johl

Words with Power, Northrop Frye, 1990

The Double Vision, Northrop Frye, 1991

The Protein Diet, Eades and Eades

A Gentlewoman in Upper Canada, H.H. Langton

Your Loving Anna, Louis Tivy

Canadian Pioneer and Fur Trader, Ada Mary Conibar

Marie of the Métis, Diane L. Commons

The Merck Manual, 14th edition

The Canadian Encyclopedia 2000, McClelland & Stewart

Funk & Wagnall's Encyclopedia

Articles

"James Evans and the Crees," *Famous Canadian Stories.* George E. Tait,

"The Fleets at War", Archibald Hurd, *The Daily Telegraph War Books, Vol. II,*

"The Social Organization of the Northern Crees", J.A.C. Kell

"James Evans", E.E. Whimster

"James Evans", Lorne Pierce

"One of a Kind", Larry Krotz, Observer, June 1973

"Away Up North," C.G. Honnor, *The Christian Guardian,* Oct. 1923

"John Wesley's Quest", J. Arundel Chapman

"Lester B. Pearson", James D. Service, *U of T Alumni Bulletin*, Apr. 1952

"The Senior Stick", R.J. McCormick, *Acta Victoriana*, May 1901

"Tommy", J.A.C. Kell, *Outlook*, Jun. 18, 1927

"No Faeries at the AGO", Jubal Brown, *The Globe and Mail*, Sept. 7, 1998

"Kindling the Fires of Friendship", J. Alex Edmison, *Saturday Night*, Jan. 5, 1957

"Forked Tongues", John Goddard, *Saturday Night*, Feb., 1988

"Wesukechak", *Journal of American Folkore, Vol. 18*

"A Canoe Trip through Northeastern Manitoba in June, 1927", Dagny Sunde

Other Sources

The Ottawa Citizen, June 20, 1998

Toronto Star, Donald Jones, Feb. 5/94

Manitoba Free Press, Aug. 29/25

Winnipeg Free Press

United Church Archives

National Archives maps